Y0-CKM-744

Canoeing for Beginners

Canoeing for Beginners

Stuart Ferguson

Arco Publishing Company, Inc.
New York

GV
783
.F47
1976

Published by Arco Publishing Company, Inc. 219 Park Avenue South, New York, N.Y. 10003

© Stuart Ferguson 1976

All rights reserved. No part of this publication may be reproduced, stored in a retrieval system, or transmitted in any form or by any means electronic, mechanical, photocopying, recording, or otherwise, without the prior written permission of the copyright owners.

Printed in Great Britain
First published in Australia by A. H. & A. W. Reed Pty. Ltd.
This edition published in Great Britain by Ward Lock Ltd., member of the Pentos Group.

Library of Congress Cataloging in Publication Data

Ferguson, Stuart.
  Canoeing for beginners.

  1. Canoes and canoeing. I. Title.
GV783.F47 1977   797.1′22   77-4341
ISBN 0-668-04319-9
ISBN 0-668-04323-7 pbk.

Rec. June 13, 1978 - 240884

PRESTON LIBRARY
VIRGINIA MILITARY INSTITUTE
LEXINGTON, VIRGINIA 24450

Contents

Acknowledgments 7

1 Canoeing 11
Canoeing as a sport—history and development

2 How to choose a canoe 14
Kayak and Canadian—design and construction

3 Your choice of canoeing 21
*Slalom—down river racing—flatwater racing
canoe sailing—touring*

4 Canoeing techniques 26
*Getting in and out of your canoe—telemark
turns—ferry gliding—repairs*

5 Paddles and paddling 40
*Double and single paddles—design and
construction—Canadian and kayak
paddle strokes*

6 Canoe safety 70
Safety on the river

7 Eskimo rolling 80
Put across—pawlata—screw

8 Canoe camping and touring 89
Equipment—packing—practical hints

9 First aid 100

Appendix

Sources of information 107

Glossary of canoeing terms 111

Acknowledgments

I would like to express my appreciation to my good friends, John Holmes and Peter Nicholls for their photographic work and Maurie Sharp for his help with sketches and the section on timber paddle construction. To Bill Andrews and Brian Frodsham my thanks for their demonstrations of paddle strokes, and to the many people who have helped me directly and indirectly to write this book.

Thus the birch canoe was builded
In the valley, by the river
In the bosom of the forest,
And the forest's life was in it.
All its mystery and magic
All the lightness of the birch tree,
All the toughness of the cedar
All the larch's supple sinew,
And it floated on the river
Like a yellow leaf in Autumn
Like a yellow water lily.

Extract from *The song of Hiawatha*,
by Henry Wadsworth Longfellow

Chapter 1 **Canoeing**

Canoeing as a sport—its history and development
When primitive man first attempted to use artificial means to
transport himself over water, he probably used a handy log
floating in the river. Although he didn't know it, he had
invented canoeing. From this first primitive mode of water
transport the raft was the most likely development, for this
introduced some stability to man's watery adventures.

The next important step in the evolution of the canoe as we
know it was the dugout. Even today in some parts of the world,
primitive peoples are still fashioning dugouts in the manner of
their ancestors. The dugout came about after man had
developed the art of making tools and starting fire. To make a
dugout a suitable tree was selected, charred with fire and then
the charred part was scraped away. A canoe of the desired
dimensions slowly took shape.

Experimentation with many different shapes revealed that a
sharp end on the canoe resulted in a much faster and more
stable vessel. The dugout canoe soon became the basis for every
type of vessel made by mankind. These have become very
elaborate and varied in their design, but the basic principle
remains the same.

In some parts of the world, boats began to appear made from
animal hides stretched over timber framework. An example of
this is the 'coracle', a circular craft which was made in the
British Isles. Perhaps a more familiar example is the Eskimo
kayak. The kayak was constructed on a timber framework with
sealskins sewn onto it. Here again many different designs and
varieties of Eskimo kayak were built to serve different purposes.

One of the most remarkable developments in the history of
canoe building was the birchbark canoe. Made from timber and
the bark of the paper birch tree, it represented one of the greatest
steps in canoe design and application. Although such canoes

varied in size, design differences were mainly in the bow and stern shape, beam and depth, and tribal markings. The length of these canoes ranged from 4 to 6 metres, but canoes up to and over 9 metres were built.

Canoeing as we know it was started in the nineteenth century by John McGregor who built himself a lightweight decked canoe which he called Rob Roy, a name which still persists to this day for a similar style of canoe manufactured in Europe. McGregor wrote many articles on canoeing and his trips, and many people built boats similar to his. The first canoe club was formed and the sport began to grow.

Over the years, many canoes have been designed, built, redesigned and redesigned again, using different materials and ideas. Today there are not a great many canvas canoes being built. The same is true of all-timber canoes, although plans are still available for boats built out of these materials. For some time aluminium was a popular material for building, but even it has been superseded since the introduction of glass-fibre and more recently carbon fibre, although the cost of the latter is prohibitive. The simplicity and speed with which a canoe can be built from glass-fibre is a great boost to the popularity of the material. Combined with its exceptional strength, it is a combination which is hard to beat.

Since World War II canoeing has developed into a major sport. The canoe slalom, started during the 1930s began to grow as a serious sport. Canoe sprint racing, always popular, became even more competitive with the introduction of the moulded veneer canoe.

Canoeing has also become a popular form of recreation, particularly in Britain and North America. Many first class designers and builders are producing a wide range of craft for both novices and experts.

Perhaps the best way to start canoeing is to make contact with the nearest canoe club. Many clubs have their own moulds for building fibreglass canoes, or have access to moulds. Building your own canoe out of glass-fibre, or any other material, is a lot of fun and certainly adds to your enjoyment when you launch your own craft. It gives you that extra sense of achievement and saves you a considerable amount of money.

Details on how to get in touch with your nearest canoe club are in the appendix at the back of the book.

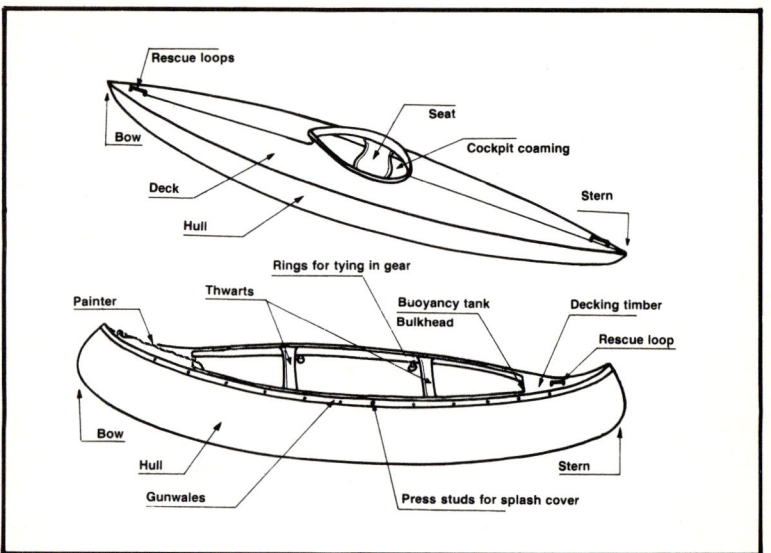

Chapter 2 How to Choose a Canoe

Whether you intend to make your own canoe or decide to buy one, there are a lot of factors to consider before you finally make the decision.

Your first consideration should be whether you want to own a Canadian canoe or a kayak. Both types have advantages and disadvantages and these should be carefully considered in view of your particular requirements.

There are no canoes that can be described accurately as all-purpose canoes. Many people have tried to produce one, and indeed many boats have been advertised as all-purpose, but canoe design and application is such that boats are built to suit specific water conditions and canoeing activities. The most important thing is hull design and we will examine this in some detail with both Canadians and kayaks.

Generally, the fastest canoes are the longest canoes, but the longer the canoe the less manoeuvrability you will have. Many racing canoes are equipped with foot-operated rudders, but in most cases even these are not very effective. So it is necessary to sacrifice some speed in order to have a canoe that will respond quickly, or at least will be capable of getting out of the sometimes tricky situations which are likely to crop up when least expected.

For a Canadian canoe, between 4.5 and 5 metres ($14\frac{1}{2}$ to $16\frac{1}{2}$ feet) is the most popular size, with a beam of approximately 81 centimetres (32 inches). This is regarded as the ideal size for two people. It will carry all the gear you will need for trips up to and over one week's duration, depending on the type of trip you are planning and consequently the type of gear you will be taking.

The biggest problem with a kayak on a long trip is the lack of room for gear and the necessity to sit in one position for long periods. This can often lead to numbness in the legs. However,

14

on a leisurely trip it is no trouble to pull into the river bank to stretch your legs and have a look around. Kayaks are generally faster than Canadians and give the paddler a greater feeling of independence. There are also a growing number of canoeists who are paddling Canadians on their own.

In Britain and Europe the two-man kayak is still quite commonly used for touring and, of course, in a specialised form for racing, but there has been a decided swing to single kayaks, particularly amongst young people, who enjoy the feeling of independence and the opportunity it provides for the exercise of a wide range of individual skills.

In America the majority of canoe tourists still use the open Canadian canoe, but for running heavy rapids on wilderness rivers the single kayak is becoming increasingly popular.

The important thing to consider when you are choosing a canoe is to know what you will primarily use it for. For touring you will require a canoe that will be relatively manoeuvrable, yet track in a straight line on open water. The average touring canoe for one man is between 4 and 4.6 metres (13 and 14½ feet) for kayaks. A one-man Canadian may be as small as 4 metres (13 feet) but should certainly be no smaller. In both cases the shorter the length the greater the beam must be to give the boat stability. And the greater the beam the greater the tendency for a boat to 'fishtail' through the water, as well as slowing the boat down.

Undoubtedly on your trips you will encounter some white water and rapids. At this time you will begin to appreciate the manoeuvrability of the slalom canoe. The slalom canoe has an entirely different purpose from the touring canoe and is available in both kayaks and Canadians. It has been designed and developed principally as a competitive boat for use on rapids, and is therefore a highly manoeuvrable boat which is not really suited to touring, although some paddlers prefer it on a trip that promises a reasonable quantity of white water.

A canoe is a displacement boat; in other words, it will not plane over the water's surface. Consequently its speed will be relative to the amount of hull surface in the water. The deeper the boat sinks in the water, the slower it will go and vice versa.

15

Other important factors relating to the speed and handling of a canoe are the hull design and its smoothness. Any projections such as 'rubbing strips' on the hull will increase the water friction, though they will certainly have a tendency to keep your canoe tracking in a straight line.

The beam of a boat is regarded as the widest point across the gunwales, and in a kayak it is the widest point from outside to outside, and not the widest point of the cockpit. There are three basic hull forms on which all boats are built. They are:

Symmetrical—the greatest beam is in the centre of the boat (Fig 1).

Swedish form—the greatest beam is aft (behind) of the centre (Fig 2).

Fish form—the greatest beam is forward of the centre (Fig 3).

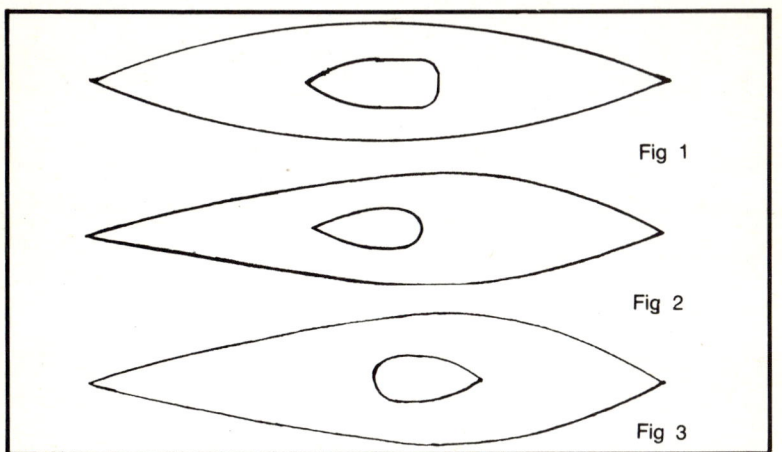

Fig 1

Fig 2

Fig 3

Most canoes are built symmetrical or have the greatest beam slightly aft of centre, which is the best position for paddling and steering with the paddle in a kayak. Of course the further aft you sit in a canoe, the easier it will be to steer with your paddle.

The fish form (greatest beam forward of centre) is a faster boat than either the symmetrical or Swedish form boats, but it is harder to handle. The steering is harder by paddle and often a foot-operated rudder is used on these boats. This can be a serious disadvantage when paddling in shallow water or in rocky rapids.

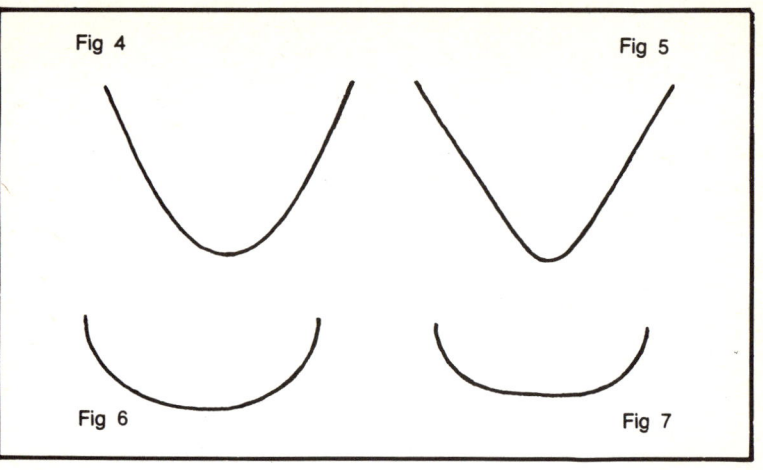

The cross-sectional shape of the hull will have considerable bearing on the stability, speed and manoeuvrability of your canoe. One of the fastest hull shapes is semi-circular in section (Fig 4) but is very unstable, as is the vee section hull (Fig 5). These particular shapes give you a minimum amount of contact with the water, so reducing friction. But they also draw more water.

The touring canoe is nearly semi-circular in cross-section (Fig 6) but it has a flattened section in the centre to increase the stability of the boat, while in length it is flat, only curving upward near the bow and stern. This means that it is a relatively fast boat and tracks well. The slalom canoe on the other hand is just the opposite. It is flat in cross-section (Fig 7) curving upwards only on the outside edges of the hull. It has a curve along the length known as 'rocker', which combined with the flat cross-section gives the boat the ability to be manoeuvred quickly in white water. The slalom canoe on flat water is slow and tends to fishtail.

Most canoes built these days are made from glass-fibre, but plans are available for canvas or vinyl skinned craft. Canvas and vinyl skin as well as plywood were used to make most canoes. Briefly the construction method for a canvas (or vinyl) skinned boat is as follows.

To the keel (this is the piece of timber that is laid along the length of the canoe in the centre of the hull) are glued and screwed the end posts for both bow and stern, and then the

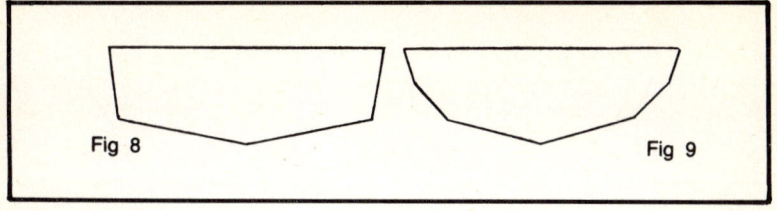

Fig 8   Fig 9

frames. These frames determine the shape of the canoe in section. To the frames are fixed the stringers, which are run from the bow and stern posts and fastened to each frame. Then the canvas is fixed, first to the bow and stern posts and then along the keel. It is then stretched over the hull and fixed at the gunwales.

The deck is covered in the same manner. After this is done, the cockpit combing is put in, together with footboards and seats, etc. The canvas is then proofed (in the case of vinyl this is not necessary). It is an advantage to have rubbing strips along the external length of the hull to protect the covering from excessive wear.

An all-ply canoe needs very little internal framework, as much of its strength lies in the toughness of the ply itself. A common design for ply canoes has a slight vee hull (Fig 8) with vertical or near vertical sides coming up to the gunwales. This type is very simple to make, but it is a cumbersome and slow canoe. However, it features excellent stability and is probably a good start for a youngster's canoeing. A modification of this design is the 'double chine' (Fig 9), a chine being the angle between two surfaces.

The design mentioned above is single chine, that is, it has only one angle between the gunwale and the keel. The double chine allows a smoother flow of water around the hull and a clearer entry into the water, as well as giving the hull a more rounded shape. Ply boats can be made from any good marine quality ply, and all joints are butted together, then glued and fixed to internal backing strips.

By far the most popular method of canoe construction is glass-fibre. With this method it is possible to build a complete kayak in one day. A Canadian takes longer because it is generally finished with a timber bow and stern decking, and timber gunwales.

A glass-fibre canoe is made in a mould, first prepared with the aid of a 'plug'. The plug is made normally on a timber framework, very similar to the internal frame of a canvas canoe. It is then covered with flywire and plaster is built up over the frame. The plaster is shaped and smoothed to the exact shape of the canoe, and finished with a coating of polyester resin to impart a hard smooth durable finish.

The building of the plug is a long, slow process, and is too time-consuming to be used for a 'one-off' boat. Its principal use is where a number of boats are to be taken off the subsequent mould. This is one of the advantages of belonging to a club, as most clubs have their own moulds which can be used by members under expert guidance.

When the plug is finished, the surface is then prepared so that the mould can be made from it. It is prepared by first waxing the surface with a non-silicone wax and then painting with release agent, which is a water soluble PVA solution. This prevents the glass-fibre sticking to the plug. At this point it should be noted that there is available a wax which incorporates a release agent. It is called Canauba wax and if this is used, the application of the PVA release agent is not necessary.

After the release agent is thoroughly dry (any trace of moisture will result in the finished article 'triping' or pitting) the Gel-coat is applied. This is the substance that forms the smooth surface on all glass-fibre products. It is usually applied with a paint roller. After this has set, or 'gone off' (approximately 20 minutes at 20°C [68°F] under ideal conditions) a layer of polyester resin is painted on, then the first layer of glass-fibre. This is then painted with more resin and worked thoroughly through the fibre. Two or three more layers or laminations of fibre and resin are applied and allowed to stand and set. This process is done separately for the deck and hull, to allow the canoes to be made in two halves and then joined.

When the mould has hardened sufficiently, it is removed from the plug and fixed onto a solid base to keep it rigid, after allowing the mould to cure. The curing time varies according to the temperature and weather conditions. Most manufacturers of glass-fibre materials will supply literature on the setting and curing times under different conditions. The mould is then ready for use. The canoes are made on the inside of the mould and the same process as described above applies.

It is sometimes desirable to glass-fibre a timber strip along the centre of the hull and deck of the canoe to strengthen them. This should be done while the canoe is in the mould and before it goes off.

After the two halves of the canoe are hard, they are put together and held with masking tape while the join is being done. This process is made easier if the canoe is supported at about chest height in rope slings. Footrests, seat and cockpit combings are then added and glassed in. Canadian canoes are often made in one piece in the mould and therefore a join is not necessary.

Carbon fibre is superior to glass fibre and although its use results in a strong boat which is extremely light in weight, it is very expensive at this stage. Glass-fibre is the best practical compromise, for it is relatively inexpensive, extremely strong and light. Repairs are easy, and done properly are as strong as the original canoe work. The colour is incorporated in the Gel-coat, so you can have any combination of colours you like by using the required pigment.

As you may now be aware, obtaining a canoe to suit you is not just a matter of going along and buying one. Shop where the people who are selling the canoes are knowledgeable in their field. Alternatively, if the canoe club scene appeals to you, go along and introduce yourself. The people there will happily provide you with the answers to most of your questions about canoes and the sport in general. Don't whatever you do be put off. Canoeing has a lot to offer and I'm sure you will enjoy it, regardless of whether you intend to canoe for recreation or competitively.

Chapter 3   Your Choice of Canoeing

This chapter deals briefly with the four main branches of the sport of canoeing. Nearly all clubs cater for the paddler who wants to specialise as well as the paddler who just wants quiet fun on the river. Canoe sport can be split into five main groups — slalom, down river racing, flatwater racing, long distance racing and touring.

Slalom

Slalom canoeing from a spectator point of view is probably the most exciting and interesting part of canoeing, depending on the slalom course and the skill of the contestants. Obviously, a slalom course that is easily mastered by all contestants with little effort won't be at all interesting either to spectators or contestants.

With a little thought and a knowledge of water behaviour, a slalom course that will test the skill of the best slalom competitor can be set up on a relatively small rapid which contains obstacles that cause water turbulence and a number of currents and eddies running in different directions and at varying speeds.

The paddler must negotiate a series of 'gates'. These are poles suspended over the rapid. The gates are numbered and must be attempted in the correct numerical sequence. By arranging the gates in a mixed up pattern on the rapid, a small section of rapid can be used to create a long and exciting course.

The gates are made of two poles hung between 1.3 and 1.4 metres (4 feet 4 inches and 4 feet 7 inches) apart, through which the paddler must pass without touching them with his boat, body or paddle. Before the start of a competition, the competitors are allowed a trial run through the course for familiarisation. During the competition the paddler is timed for each of his two runs and penalised for touching, missing, or failing to attempt gates. The object of a slalom competition is to negotiate the course without incurring any penalty points. After a paddler's second run his points are totalled for both runs and the best run point score is used for judging purposes.

If two paddlers tie on any one score, then the paddler with the lowest time for his run is the place getter. Should a paddler capsize during his run, the run is disqualified unless he manages to roll back up and continue the course. During a slalom event the paddler must wear a buoyancy vest and crash hat. His boat must be adequately buoyant so that it will float level in the water after a capsize. All competitors must be good swimmers.

The slalom kayak for competition purposes has certain size regulations: minimum length 4 metres (13 feet), minimum beam or breadth 60 centimetres (24 inches). While the boat has to be highly manoeuvrable it must also be fast and stable. In canoe design these are contradictory qualities, so the resulting boat must be a compromise.

The slalom canoeist is a specialist to a high degree. He must have complete control over his boat, have a thorough knowledge of water behaviour, a good sense of timing and supreme confidence in fast-moving water. All these qualities must react as one. A canoeist's balance and technique are constantly changing with his speed and position on the course. Every gate is a new challenge and a changing set of circumstances. Every obstacle on the course requires a different technique and stroke. Every eddy requires an adjustment of balance.

These are the conditions he must master while still concentrating on a definite course. Slalom canoeing requires something extra from a canoeist, and as a result it will not appeal to everyone. However, an attempt at a slalom course will be beneficial to all canoeists, and will give you some indication of how much skill you really have. Your local club secretary will no doubt have all the details of the club's next slalom course and would be very happy to give you the necessary information.

Down river racing
A down river race is usually held on a rapid river and presents a

challenge to all competitors. The down river racing enthusiast must combine some of the skills of the slalom canoeist with the endurance of a racing canoeist.

Like the slalom paddler, he must be able to read the river to enable him to plan his best path through a certain set of obstacles. Speed is essential for he is not competing against a clock, but against the competitor behind him, who is only waiting for one error in judgment to enable him to slip past.

The down river racing boat must be fast and lightweight. It must also be strong enough to take the knocks and jars of this type of canoeing, while still retaining some degree of manoeuvrability. It is usually built with a deep rounded or vee hull for speed, but it is shorter than a flatwater racing boat. Because of the type of water raced over, the down river racing boat is steered by paddle. Attaching a foot-operated rudder would be of doubtful value because of the danger of snagging it and having it knocked or pulled off. The paddler must possess a fine sense of balance as these boats are very unstable, mainly because of the shape of the hull in cross-section.

Down river racing is an exciting sport, which is growing rapidly in popularity wherever there are rivers providing torrent conditions.

Flatwater racing

In flatwater racing the courses used are 500, 1,000 and 10,000 metres for men; 500 metres for women. For the juniors (those under eighteen years of age on January 1st of the year of competition), the course is 500 and 1,000 metres for boys and 500 metres for women.

The racing canoeist must possess a high degree of technical skill and spend a good proportion of his or her time in training. The two major factors that contribute towards making a champion are ability and power. Ability includes such things as technical skill in the stroke, speed of stroke and tactics while racing. Power factors are strength, stamina and a high degree of physical efficiency.

The racing canoeist must do a good deal of power training on land as well as in the canoe. Land training includes running, weight lifting and calisthenics to improve muscle tone, movement and body mobility. Canoe training includes paddling technique, start and finish sprints, relaxed paddling and power paddling.

Paddling technique is fairly standard among racing paddlers, although there may be some slight variations between individuals. Basically it involves a high sitting position and a long paddle stroke, with the paddle blade close to the boat. Technique can often be improved by shifting body position slightly or altering the paddling position of the hands. Seek out the advice of an expert on these points. He will be able to give some helpful advice and pointers to improve your technique. Never underestimate the importance of power and strength, because when the skill of paddlers is evenly matched, the stronger man will win.

The racing boat is of major importance. No matter how good you are, a poor boat will rob you of victory. The International Canoe Federation has laid down specifications for length, breadth and weight of racing boats and these are set out below. The letter 'K' indicates a kayak and the letter 'C' indicates a Canadian. The number following each letter indicates the number in the crew.

International Canoe Federation specifications

Model	Maximum length	Minimum breadth	Minimum weight
K.1.	520 cm	51 cm	12 kg
K.2.	650 cm	55 cm	18 kg
K.4.	1100 cm	60 cm	30 kg
C.1.	520 cm	75 cm	16 kg
C.2.	650 cm	75 cm	20 kg

These specifications are rigidly adhered to and all boats are checked before the start of a championship event.

Until recently racing boats have been generally of timber construction, smooth and highly polished to reduce friction. However, the high cost of suitable timber and improved techniques in glass-fibre construction are leading to an increasing use of this and similar materials. Racing craft are built with a deep rounded or vee hull and in the case of the kayak are fitted with a rudder either at the stern or under the stern. This facilitates manoeuvring as the paddler is putting all his effort into speed.

Long Distance Racing (Canoe Marathon)

Long distance racing is to flatwater racing as cross country running is to track running. The distances raced may be anything from 20 to 200 kilometres (13 to 123 miles) or more, and the events may be single stage or multistage and extending over several days. The features that really distinguish long distance events from flatwater or downriver races are the hazards and obstacles which may include stretches of shallow water, rapids, weirs to be negotiated or portaged, locks calling for a portage, even rough water on sea, estuary or lake. The winner is the one making the best total paddling time. Races are held for a variety of boat classes including the flatwater racing boats and a variety of distances.

Canoe Sailing

Although many canoeists have rigged up a simple sail on their paddling canoes, the true sailing canoe is specifically designed for this form of propulsion and has evolved over more than 100 years. The sailing canoes used in international competition are amongst the fastest single-handed and single-hulled vessels in the world, and are a World Championship class in the I.C.F. There are also national classes in the various countries which practise canoe sailing, and in North America there is a touring class using Canadian canoes fitted with leeboards and steered by the paddle. This branch of canoeing is particularly popular in Britain, Sweden, Germany and the United States.

Touring

Touring probably attracts most people to the sport initially and for this reason there is a chapter on touring and canoe camping elsewhere in the book.

Chapter 4   Canoeing Techniques

One of the biggest problems confronting novice canoeists is
finding the easiest method of getting into and out of canoes,
both from the bank and from deep water. It must be
remembered that no matter how strongly canoes are built they
will only take a certain amount of strain. For this reason a
canoe, Canadian or kayak, should never be stepped into while
its bow or stern is resting on a bank, that is, bow on the bank,
stern in the water, and fresh air in between. As far as possible
the canoe should be in water deep enough to float with your
weight in it, before you get in.

Deep water landing
Canadian canoe
To get into a canoe from a deep water landing such as a wharf,
or from a bank where the river bed drops away sharply, place
one foot lightly into the centre of the boat. Keep the other foot
on shore to maintain the canoe in position then bend forward
and grip both gunwales with your hands and bring your other
leg inboard and either sit or kneel down.

Kayak
Entry into a kayak from a wharf or steep bank is basically the
same technique as for the Canadian canoe. It might, however,
be more convenient to squat down on your haunches before
putting your foot in the kayak, as kayaks are generally more
unstable than Canadians.

Shallow water
Canadian canoe
The same method as for a deep water landing is used to enter a
canoe from shallow water, except that the foot left on shore can
be used to push the canoe into deeper water before being

brought inboard. The technique for two men entering a canoe from shallow water is for the stern hand to enter first and sit or kneel down. The bow hand then pushes the canoe into deeper water and enters the canoe himself.

Kayak
Entry in shallow water is accomplished by floating the kayak and gripping opposite gunwales with both hands and stepping quickly into the centre of the boat. Follow with the other foot and slide your legs under the decking. Alternatively, if the cockpit is large enough, sit down first, then slide your legs under the decking. Two-man kayaks can be entered in much the same way as two-man Canadians.

Deepwater midstream entry
Canadian canoe
If the canoe is empty, grip the left gunwale with your left hand, and the opposite gunwale with your right hand, then lean the canoe towards you. Throw your body weight into the canoe, and at the same time give a strong scissor kick with your legs. Roll over onto your back and swing your legs inboard. Resume normal paddling position.

Canadian self-rescue Stage 1

Stage 2
Stage 3

28

Stage 4

In the event that two canoeists have to enter, one man can support himself while at the same time steadying the canoe on the opposite side. If the canoe is full of water, and provided that it is fitted with adequate buoyancy, entry is quite easy. Just swim in and paddle the canoe full of water back to the bank.

A capsized Canadian canoe can be Eskimo rolled full of water quite easily, and then paddled to shore full of water. The roll is basically the same as the 'put across' roll for kayaks detailed in chapter 7.

29

Canadian roll—after capsize, paddle is thrust out and up to surface

Canadian roll, using a technique similar to the 'put across' roll

Kayak

If a kayak is empty, by far the easiest method of entering is over the stern. From a position at the rear of the boat, take hold of the stern, push it under water between your legs, and then lie forward along the deck. With outstretched arms and lying on the deck, grasp the back of the gunwale. Pull yourself along the deck and sit just behind the cockpit, then bring legs inboard into the cockpit, and slide into your seat. Now resume normal paddling position. If the kayak is full of water, either swim and tow it to shore or sit in it and paddle it to shore. A capsized kayak full of water can be Eskimo rolled, but it will be very unstable in the water.

Kayak self-rescue   Starting position
Stage 2

Stage 3
Stage 4

The telemark turn

The telemark turn is a fast turn, usually executed in a kayak, that relies on water resistance to the paddle blade (see 'Sculling for support' in chapter 5). It is used extensively in slalom canoeing, but has many practical uses in ordinary canoeing practices, as well as in surf canoeing. It is particularly useful for turning quickly into an eddy from a fast flowing current, turning into a landing spot from out of a fast current, and breaking out and over a wave in the surf.

The telemark can be practised in quiet water by paddling forward and building up speed. Push your paddle out towards the stern on the right hand side (to turn right) with your arm fully extended. In the same movement, slap your paddle blade down flat on the water's surface with the leading edge up slightly. Then heel the kayak over sharply to the right and support your weight on the paddle. To right the kayak with your weight still on the paddle, sweep the blade in an arc on the surface until it is abeam, then press down on the blade and at the same time flick the kayak upright with your hips.

When doing a low telemark, your body should be leaning forward while your left hand is approximately at chin height. When doing a high telemark your body will lean forward slightly, while your left hand will be above your head. The telemark turn should be practised on right and left hand sides until it is perfected.

Low telemark turn, with paddler leaning into turn

High telemark turn. Paddler leaning into turn and stern of kayak swinging round

Ferry gliding

The ferry glide, both upstream and downstream, is a technique that should be mastered before attempting any rapid river trips. The ferry glide is used for moving sideways across a current, while remaining stationary in the current. Imagine that you are moving downstream in a swift current. After paddling around one obstacle you are faced with another, so close to you that to attempt to turn your canoe would cause the current to sweep you broadside into it. You should immediately back paddle as this will hold you stationary in the current.

Now swing the stern of your canoe slightly in the direction you wish to go to avoid the obstruction. The current pushing against the diagonally exposed side of the canoe will push it sideways across the river. Allow your canoe to travel sideways across the current until you are faced with a clear run, then resume paddling forward (Fig 10).

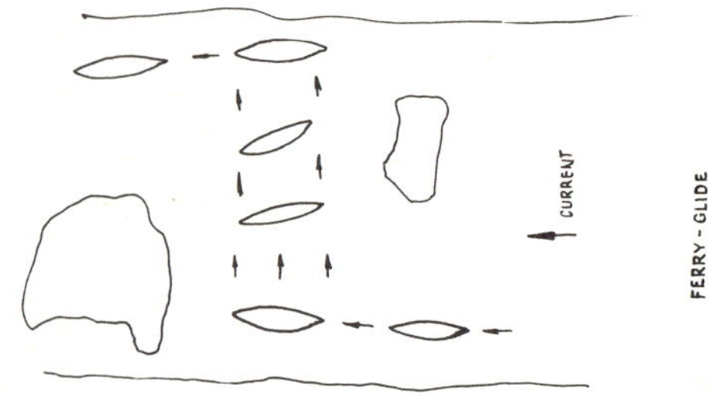

Fig 10

The theory behind the ferry glide can perhaps be demonstrated best by paddling upstream. Paddle just fast enough to hold your canoe against the current. Angle the bow of your canoe in the direction you wish to go. The current will push you across the stream.

On many occasions it is desirable to paddle directly across a swift current. To do this you must angle the bow slightly upstream and paddle across the current on the downstream side of the canoe, at the same time leaning downstream so that the effect of the water rushing under the hull will keep you buoyant. Do not lean the canoe upstream. If you do the water will rush onto the deck and cause a capsize.

The only exception to this rule is when you are bow hand in a Canadian. In this case you would do a bow draw stroke on the upstream side of the canoe in order to keep your bow facing upstream. The stern paddler paddles on the downstream side. If the bow hand paddles on the downstream side, the force of water will push the canoe onto your paddle with a possible capsize as a result.

Repairs

No matter what material your canoe is constructed from, some day it will be in need of repair. Rapid water trips are very exciting, but they often lead to repairs having to be carried out on the river bank. Every canoeist should carry a repair kit to suit the material of his canoe.

A typical repair kit for canvas or vinyl covered canoes and ply canoes would consist of the following essential materials:

A good quality waterproof adhesive—a contact adhesive is
  excellent
A quantity of proofed canvas, or vinyl
Glasspaper, medium coarse
Sailmaker's needle and thread—a must for canvas and vinyl
  skinned canoes
Heavy plastic adhesive tape

Repairs to canvas or ply canoes can be effected easily and quickly, provided the correct preliminary steps are taken. In all cases the surfaces to be repaired must be clean and dry. In the case of a very small tear or split in canvas or ply, plastic tape applied to a clean dried surface will usually prove satisfactory.

36

A long tear in canvas should be sewn before a patch is applied.

The same patching procedure applies for both canvas and ply canoes. Cut a patch of suitable size, allowing for a good overlap. Apply adhesive to the canoe and then the patch material. If you are using a contact adhesive, allow the first coat to dry, then apply another coat. Allow to dry before pressing the patch into position.

A ply canoe may require a patch placed inside the canoe as well as an external one. It is a good idea to 'key' the surface of the canoe with glasspaper before applying adhesive, especially if, in the case of ply, the surface is painted or varnished.

Glass-fibre repairs
An adequate repair kit is a must for canoes moulded from glass-fibre. In the main repairs will be to small cracks. Glass-fibre has a tendency to crush on impact and the fibre, more often than not, will hold the shattered resin in place. Large holes nevertheless are not altogether uncommon, so a good quantity of glass-fibre mat and resin should be carried.

A glass-fibre repair kit should consist of the following essential items:

226 grams (8 ounces) (approx. 1 x 0.4 metre [3 feet 3 inches by 1 ft 6 inches]) of chopped strand
42-gram ($1\frac{1}{2}$-ounce) mat
340-453 grams (12-16 ounces) of polyester resin in a clean plastic container
M.E.K.P. catalyst (hardener). It will probably be convenient to carry about 20 millilitres (about $\frac{8}{10}$ of a fluid ounce) in a small plastic bottle
A piece of a broken hacksaw blade, or a medium piece of glasspaper
One 25-millimetre (1 inch) paint brush
Parsley cutter if desired
Heavy gauge adhesive plastic tape

Small cracks in glass-fibre can be temporarily repaired by thoroughly drying the area and applying tape. If you are paddling in shallow water, however, this will not be satisfactory, and a glass-fibre patch will have to be applied.

Ideally a patch should be applied inside the canoe, but if for any reason this is not possible, apply an external patch, and don't make it too bulky.

To apply a patch internally or externally, the procedure is the same. First make sure the area around the break is clean and perfectly dry. Key the area with the hacksaw blade or glasspaper. This allows the resin to create a firm bond. Mix the resin and catalyst together. The normal ratio is 5 millilitres ($\frac{1}{8}$ fluid ounce) to 453 grams (16 ounces) of resin. For a small amount of resin the mixing ratio will be very difficult to calculate, as only a small amount of catalyst will be needed, so the actual measurement will have to be purely guesswork. This is where experience always helps.

Paint around the break area with resin, and saturate the glass with resin also. Be careful not to use too much resin. Saturate in this instance means to work the resin through the glass mat. Apply the patch to the break and work with a parsley cutter or paint brush. The time needed for the resin to harden will depend on the amount of catalyst used, and the prevailing weather conditions. Do not use too much catalyst to speed up hardening time, or a very poor quality patch will result. Under good conditions the patch will harden within 30 minutes.

Useful hints Clean up tools with cold or cool soapy water. Work soap deep into the bristles of your paint brush to prevent hardening. A damp paint brush should never be used. If a damp paint brush is all that's available, dip it in acetone and then allow the acetone to dry out. If acetone is used to clean resin from your hands, wash your hands with soapy water immediately after. Continued use of acetone for hand cleaning can cause dermatitis.

Trim glass-fibre while it is still 'green' with a sharp knife or chisel. Cured glass-fibre can be filed or sanded easily. Catalyst should be added to Gel-coat in ratio of 8-10 millilitres (about $\frac{1}{4}$ fluid ounce) of a catalyst to 453 grams (16 ounces) of Gel-coat.

Hardened resin on parsley cutters can be burnt off. When building a canoe, estimate the total amount of resin to be used, measure it into a separate drum and pigment the total amount. By doing this you will avoid the possibility of having a canoe of many different colour shades.

A glass-fibre repair kit, including chopped strand glass-fibre mat, polyester resin, catalyst, broken hacksaw blade, roller, mug and plastic measuring cup

Chapter 5   Paddles and Paddling

In order to get the best performance and the most enjoyment from your canoe, it is very important to use the correct paddle. There are many different types. Traditionally, Canadian canoes are propelled with single bladed paddles, and indeed these must be used in all forms of competition. It is important that your paddle is bought or made to suit you, and consideration must be given to blade size, length and weight. As a general rule, your paddle should, when standing upright, come level with your eyes. This of course will vary with the individual, so a wise course is to try several different paddles and then pick one to suit yourself.

Kayak paddles are double bladed with the blades generally turned at right angles to each other. However, you can still buy paddles with the blades in the same plane. These should be avoided where possible, as the advantages of feathered or 90-degree blades are great. Many paddlers prefer to feather their own blades at 75 degrees, but this is a matter of personal choice, and it can only be made by experience. Feathered paddles are easier to use, give greater control of your boat, increase your paddling power, and offer less resistance to the wind.

The length of any paddle is strictly regulated for competition purposes, but for normal use your paddle can be made to suit yourself. A good guide is to stand the paddle in an upright position. If you can curl your fingers over the uppermost blade to the first knuckle, this will probably be a suitable length. Here again experience will be your best guide.

Paddle blades are either straight or curved. The type you choose will depend on the type of water you are intending to paddle in, and the branch of the sport you prefer. For straight forward flatwater paddling, touring or racing, the curved blade is better, because it tends to scoop the water, giving greater

40

speed for the same amount of power expended on a straight bladed paddle.

If you intend to build your own canoe you will probably build your own paddles as well. It doesn't matter whether you prefer timber or glass-fibre as a building material; excellent paddles can be made from either.

Glass-fibre paddle construction

Glass-fibre paddles are usually made on an aluminium extruded shaft. This is fairly easy to obtain, but exercise some care when purchasing it. First determine a comfortable diameter. Usually from 29 to 32 millimetres ($1\frac{1}{10}$ to $1\frac{2}{10}$ inches) is suitable. Then make sure that the gauge of the aluminium is heavy enough to withstand the stresses that will be placed on it. Determine the overall length of the paddle, then subtract 150 to 200 millimetres (6-8 inches) from this and cut your shaft to suit. Remove any burrs and firmly plug the open ends with cork or timber.

The next step is to obtain a mould. If you have to make one, there are various methods available. One of the easiest methods is to cut a piece of masonite or similar material to the shape you require for your finished blade. Assuming you are using a shaft with an external diameter of 32 millimetres ($1\frac{2}{10}$ inches) you will require an extra length of shaft, long enough to go within 76 to 100 millimetres (3 to 4 inches) of the end of your blade. Mark a centre line along the length of this piece on both sides with a pencil.

Now cut a slot in the centre of the masonite the length of this piece of shaft and wide enough for the shaft to be a neat press fit into it. Press the piece of shaft into it so that the centre lines you marked are flush with the surface on the shiny side of the masonite. Fix the shaft in position on the bottom side with scrap glass-fibre and resin. You now have a male mould.

At this stage, you can do one of two things. You can either make two half blades on the mould, and put them together around your paddle shaft, after waxing and applying a release agent (see chapter 2), or you can make one half blade and by laying your prepared shaft into it, laminate glass-fibre over the top. Take care that you remove all traces of

41

wax, and release if used, from the inside of your blade's halves, or half as the case may be, before joining. Use either polyester thinners or acetone for the purpose.

By using a male mould, your finished blades will have the texture of the glass-fibre on the external sides of the blade. This is only of minor importance, as the male mould is much easier to make than a female one. Extra strength can be imparted to the blade by applying extra laminations of glass-fibre to the extreme ends. A popular idea amongst paddlers is to fold and rivet a strip of lightweight copper over the tips of the blades to prolong life. Because of the buildup of aluminium oxide on paddle shafts it is advisable to clear lacquer the shaft before use. This of course will only be necessary if the shaft is not anodised. If you decide you do not wish to make your paddle, specialist shops now have a good range of paddles and replacement blades.

Timber paddle construction—curved blade

If possible, use spruce and ash timber for paddles. This is usually obtainable from the larger timber merchants specialising in boat building.

Glue to be used is Resorcinal Formaldehyde (Resibond). This glue stains red and care is essential when using it. A clear non-staining glue of Resibond Standard may be used if desired.

Buy a length of 38-millimetre square ($1\frac{1}{2}$ inches square) spruce for the shaft. Although involving much more work a stronger and better job can be obtained from sandwiching a length of 38 x 6 millimetre ($1\frac{1}{2}$ x $\frac{2}{10}$ inches) ash between two 16-millimetre ($\frac{6}{10}$ inches) layers of spruce. Glue and clamp well (Fig 11).

This size timber will make a shaft suitable for a large hand and a strong arm. Sizes may be reduced to suit the individual.

Laminations of 38-millimetre wide x 29-millimetre ($1\frac{1}{2}$ x $1\frac{2}{10}$ inches) thick spruce and ash 45 centimetres (18 inches) long are glued to one end to form the paddle blades. These should be alternated, ash to spruce etc. Six-millimetre ($\frac{4}{10}$ inch) laminations of cedar can also be included to enhance the appearance, though the final laminate should not exceed 22 centimetres (9 inches)

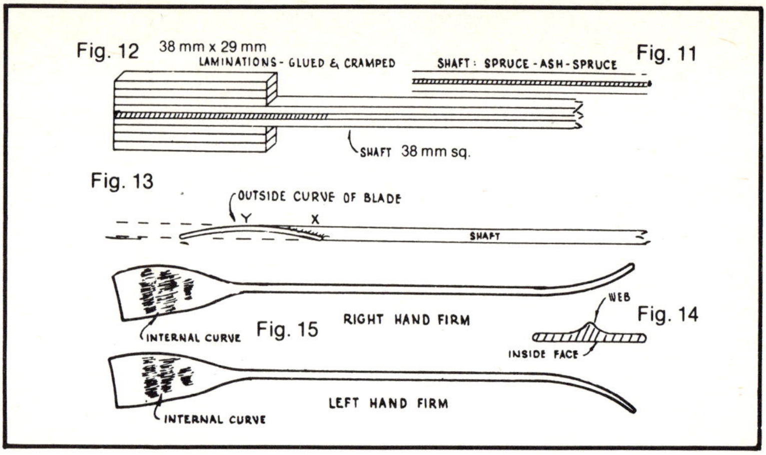

Fig. 12 38 mm x 29 mm LAMINATIONS - GLUED & CRAMPED   SHAFT : SPRUCE - ASH - SPRUCE   Fig. 11

SHAFT 38 mm sq.

Fig. 13

OUTSIDE CURVE OF BLADE
Y   X
SHAFT

INTERNAL CURVE   Fig. 15   RIGHT HAND FIRM   WEB   Fig. 14

INSIDE FACE

LEFT HAND FIRM

INTERNAL CURVE

width with the hardest timber forming the outside
laminations (Fig 12). The curve of the blade is now
marked on the 38-millimetre ($1\frac{1}{2}$ inch) thick face or edge
of the laminations, the curved back of the blade and the
tip in a straight line extended from the shaft (Fig 13).

Roughly trim to shape with a band saw and then mark out
the plan shape of the paddle and trim also. It is advisable to
have this shape in template form on cardboard first (Fig 13). To
finish the job off, use a spokeshave and rasp. The paddle shaft is
best rounded with a plane except where it blends into the blade.
Use a spokeshave here. It is important to form a strengthening
web at 'X' in Figure 13, and blend it through to the peak of the
curve at 'Y'. In cross-section it should look like Figure 14, and
in plan it should look like Figure 15.

Curved feathered blades are made either for left hand firm or
right hand firm paddlers. When you are paddling, either your
left hand or your right hand is tight on the shaft, to turn the
shaft back and forth to counteract the 90-degree feather. Take
care in determining which you are before making your paddle.
In order to control your boat under all conditions, you must
have a knowledge of all the basic paddling strokes. All paddle
strokes must be learnt, and their application fully understood,
before you can efficiently control your boat. Paddling is not a
haphazard business. Each stroke has a function and is used in
specific paddling situations.

Canadian canoe paddle strokes
Bow stroke
The basis of all paddle strokes is the bow stroke. It is used by the
bow and stern hand for forward paddling, in a C.2. (two-man
Canadian), or used by the paddler from amidships in a C.1.
(one-man Canadian). To execute the stroke correctly take the
grip or handle of the paddle in one hand and with the other
hand grasp the shaft as far down as you can comfortably reach
with your arm fully outstretched. The blade will enter the water
at approximately 45 degrees off vertical in front of you. The
hand on the shaft pulls directly back, while the hand on the
grip pushes forward from the shoulder until the midpoint is
reached. The movement is continued through to
approximately 45 degrees behind you. The paddle is lifted clear
of the water at this point, to begin the stroke again. The stroke
should be made close to and alongside the canoe. The power in
this stroke (as with most others) is equally distributed through
both arms.

Bow stroke—starting position

Bow stroke—mid-point
Bow stroke—finish position

Backwater stroke

The backwater stroke is used to hold the canoe against a current, to stop the forward motion of the canoe on still water, or to move the canoe backwards. The paddle movements are the reverse of those of the bow stroke.

Backwater stroke—starting position

Backwater stroke—mid-point

Backwater stroke—finish position

J stroke

The J stroke is most commonly used by a single paddler in a Canadian canoe and sometimes by the stern paddler in a C.2. for steering. If used by a paddler in a C.1., it enables him to paddle on one side only, and keep his canoe on a straight course. The C.1. paddler usually sits or kneels in the centre, or just aft of centre. The position aft of centre is the best position for the J stroke, as it allows greater purchase on the water.

J stroke—starting position

J stroke—mid-point

J stroke—finish position

The stroke is started in the same position as the bow stroke, and carried through to the midpoint. At this point the paddle blade is turned out, away from the side of the canoe to form the 'tail' of the J. The J stroke used from the centre of the canoe is started in the same position, but as the paddle reaches the midpoint it should be pulled in under the side of the canoe and finished off the same way as the J stroke described above.

Trail stroke
The trail stroke is used for the same purpose as the J stroke, but because of the resultant loss of power in using this stroke, it is not as popular. It is a useful stroke to practise, however, and it may be found convenient to use when paddling with a crosswind, or when the wind is three-quarters on to the bow or stern.

It starts in the same position as the bow stroke and carries through to the midpoint. At the finish point, the paddle blade is turned so that it is in a vertical position in the water, and trailed for a few seconds. The actual time depends on the prevailing conditions.

Draw stroke
The basic function of the draw stroke is to move the canoe sideways through the water. This can be necessary for a variety of reasons, such as pulling into or away from a deepwater landing or pulling alongside or away from another canoe. It is done from the centre of the canoe in the case of a C.1. or from bow and stern in the case of a C.2.

The paddle is placed in the water abeam of the paddler, and as far out as can be reached comfortably with your lower arm outstretched. Then pull towards the side of the canoe, finishing vertical but not touching the side. The blade is then lifted clear of the water and returned to the starting position. The draw stroke may be used to draw the canoe sideways to clear obstacles in moving water, particularly in C.1. paddling.

Sculling draw
The sculling draw is used to move the canoe sideways through the water like a draw stroke. The advantage of the sculling draw is that the paddle is not lifted from the water.

Place the paddle vertically in the water at a comfortable distance from the side of the canoe, with your lower arm nearly

Trail stroke—starting position

Trail stroke—mid-point
Trail stroke—finish position

outstretched. The paddle is then moved through the water in an arc of 45 degrees forward, and 45 degrees astern of the paddler. Remember to keep the leading edge of the paddle blade tilted slightly up as the blade moves backwards and forwards. While the blade is in motion, the lower arm will be pulling the blade towards the paddler. In actual fact, the paddler will be pulling himself towards the paddle blade.

Pushover stroke
The pushover stroke is the direct opposite of the draw stroke and pushes the canoe away from the paddle. It may be used in conjunction with the draw stroke.

Bow draw
The bow draw is a manoeuvring stroke used by the bow paddler in moving water. Its main purpose is to swing the bow clear of obstructions, or to bring the bow into the current. It is particularly useful where the canoe is moving slowly, or where the canoe is only moving at the same speed as the current. It is used on the same side as the paddler is paddling, and no alteration of grip is necessary.

The paddle blade is placed in the water ahead of the paddler, and as far away from the side of the canoe as can be reached comfortably. It is often necessary to lean forward over the bow of the canoe in order to increase the effectiveness of this stroke. The blade is pulled back to the paddler, but should not touch the side of the canoe. This stroke will effectively pull the bow diagonally towards the starting point of the paddle.

Cross bow draw
The cross bow draw is used for the same purpose and under the same conditions as the bow draw. The difference is that it is used on the opposite side of the canoe from the side the paddler is paddling on. The only alteration in grip will be to move the lower hand further up the shaft to avoid knocking your fingers on the gunwales.

From the normal paddling position swing the paddle across the bow of the canoe and into the water on the other side. In this position a draw stroke is then done.

Bow rudder
The bow rudder is used when the bow of the canoe has to be

Sculling draw stroke—starting position

Sculling draw stroke—mid-point
Sculling draw stroke—finish position

Bow draw stroke—starting position

Bow draw stroke—finish position

turned sharply towards the side on which the bow man is paddling. It is particularly useful where the canoe is moving faster than the current or moving fast over still water.

The paddle blade is placed vertically in the water in front of the paddler and angled towards the direction you want the bow to go. This angle can be increased or decreased, depending on how fast you want the bow to turn and, of course, the strength of the paddler. The paddle should not be placed at a great angle from the bow at high speed, or there will be a tendency for the paddle to be pulled violently from the paddler's hands. Once in position, the paddle must be held solidly until the manoeuvre is completed.

Cross bow rudder

The cross bow rudder is done on the opposite side of the canoe from the normal paddling side. The grip on the paddle is not changed, as the paddle is swung over the bow into the water on the other side. The procedure for bow rudder is used. Both bow rudder and cross bow rudder can be used by a C.1. paddler from the centre of the canoe.

Sweep stroke

The sweep stroke is used for a variety of reasons but mainly to achieve the pivot turn, which turns the canoe without any unnecessary movement. If the canoe is stationary, two or three sweep strokes will take it through a complete circle on the spot. The sweep stroke is a useful manoeuvring stroke which enables the paddler to effect quick course changes with a minimum of lost time. It also helps to hold a straight course in crosswinds.

The sweep stroke can be used as a complete 180-degree sweep, or partial sweep by a C.1. paddler sitting or kneeling in or slightly aft of centre in his canoe, depending on how much of a turn you wish to make. Paddlers sitting bow and stern on a C.2. should make only 90-degree sweeps. That is, the bow paddler sweeps from forward through 90 degrees to abeam of his own position, and the stern paddler sweeps from abeam his position to 90 degrees astern. Any more than a 90-degree sweep will tend to negate the effectiveness of the first 90 degrees.

For solo (C.1.) paddlers the sweep stroke is started with the paddle blade held vertically in the water directly ahead of the paddler, then swept through 180 degrees to a position directly astern of the paddler. The first 90 degrees pushes the bow away from the paddle, while the second 90 degrees pulls the stern towards the paddle.

Cross bow draw stroke—starting position

Cross bow draw stroke—finish position

Bow rudder

Cross bow rudder

56

Sweep stroke—starting position

Sweep stroke—finish position

Reverse sweep

The reverse sweep is accomplished by starting directly astern and sweeping the paddle through 180 degrees or less, depending on how much turn is needed. The paddle can be returned to the starting position by lifting clear of the water or by feathering the blade under water and slicing it back to the starting position.

With a basic knowledge of these paddling strokes, you will probably find many ways to refine them and so suit your own individual paddling style. They should all be learnt correctly and practised regularly if competence is to be achieved. There are quite a few other paddling strokes, many of them only slightly different from the ones described in this chapter, but they should not be attempted until the basic strokes are known, well practised and understood.

Correct position adopted for paddling on one knee

Position adopted when paddling with wind astern

Position adopted when paddling into a headwind

Paddling positions

While many Canadian canoes, particularly C.2.s, are fitted
with seats, a great many canoeists prefer to kneel or alternate
their positions for comfort. Kneeling down on both knees and
sitting on your heels is a comfortable position for touring. It
has another advantage in that it lowers your centre of gravity,
thus decreasing the risk of a capsize. The main problem with
this position is that it is not conducive to powerful paddling
strokes. The kneeling up position, either on both knees or on
one knee, allows comfortable touring, and also enables you to
put maximum power into paddle strokes without changing
position.

Paddling into or with the wind in a Canadian canoe can be a
trying business. One way to ease the problem, particularly
when paddling a C.1., is to sit as far astern as possible when
paddling with the wind behind you, and as far forward as
possible when paddling into a headwind.

Launching canoes

When launching a Canadian canoe from a wharf, first place the canoe parallel with the wharf edge, stand behind it and then grip the gunwale edge nearest to you. Lift the canoe onto your knees. Walk forward in this position and lower the canoe into the water. Bringing the canoe ashore onto a wharf would be the reverse of this procedure.

Launching from a wharf   Stage 1

Stage 2
Stage 3

Kayak paddle strokes

While a large percentage of strokes are common to both kayak and Canadian paddlers, there are of course a number of strokes used particularly by kayak paddlers. This is more pronounced in slalom or rapid river paddling.

Forward paddling

This stroke, like the bow stroke for Canadian canoes, is the basic kayak paddling stroke. The paddle is gripped with both hands on the shaft, approximately shoulder width apart. The hands may be placed a little more than shoulder width apart if necessary, depending on the paddler's comfort. The blades enter the water with the lower paddle edge angled slightly forward. You will find this will occur quite naturally.

The stroke starts approximately 45 degrees ahead of the paddler, and finishes when the paddler's hand is in line with his hip or just a little astern. Power exerted too far behind the hip line is wasted. The stroke is made on alternate sides of the canoe to maintain a straight course.

Backwatering

This is the reverse of forward paddling. It is used while executing the downstream ferry glide manoeuvre, for paddling backwards, or to slow down or stop forward motion.

Forward paddling—left hand paddle stroke

Draw stroke—starting position

Draw stroke
The draw stroke is used to draw the kayak sideways through the water. Its use is common in slalom canoeing in conjunction with or in place of the telemark turn or bow rudder techniques. Because it moves the kayak over sideways instead of turning it, this stroke can be used to clear an obstruction completely, whereas a telemark or bow rudder would bring the kayak broadside on to the same obstruction. It also has the advantage that it can be used in confined waters. The technique is the same as that for Canadian canoes. The blade is placed vertically in the water abeam of the paddler, and at a comfortable distance of say 0.6 to 1 metre (2 to 3 feet) away. The lower arm pulls in, while the higher arm pushes, thus pulling the kayak towards the blade.

Draw stroke—finish. Paddle positioned to return to start

Sculling draw

The function of the sculling draw stroke is the same as for the draw stroke. Its advantage is in the fact that there is less wasted time and effort. The paddle blade does not leave the water until the manoeuvre is completed. The blade is placed in the water in the same position as for the draw stroke, and is then moved to and fro through an arc 45 degrees ahead and 45 degrees astern of the paddler. On the backward and forward movements the leading edge of the blade is tilted slightly up to keep it mounting towards the surface. At the same time as the paddle is sweeping to and fro, the paddler's lower arm is pulling, and his upper arm is pushing, thereby drawing the kayak towards the blade.

Sculling draw—photo shows paddle at mid-point of return stroke. Note leading edge of blade

Sculling draw—paddle blade at mid-point of forward stroke

Sculling for support

As the name implies, this stroke is used to support the paddler and kayak while the paddler is leaning over. The sculling action is the same as for the sculling draw stroke, except that the blade is moved much faster and nearly parallel to the water's surface. The leading edge of the blade is still tilted up so that it is always actively mounting towards the surface, so supporting the weight of the paddler.

Sculling for support. Note leading edge of paddle tilted up for forward sweep

Sculling for support—end of forward sweep

Slap support

Slap support

The slap support is used to regain balance when faced with the possibility of a capsize. The technique is to simply bring the paddle blade down in a hard fast slap. While your weight is supported momentarily by the water resistance of the flat paddle blade, right the kayak with a quick hip movement, and at the same time regain your balance.

Bow rudder

The bow rudder is used to make a fast turn. It will only work effectively if the kayak is moving at speed on still water, or moving faster than the current in moving water. The bow rudder should be practised a great deal, as its use by inexperienced canoeists can easily result in a capsize.

The technique is to place the paddle blade in the water vertically ahead of the paddler, and at an angle to the fore and aft line of the kayak, on the side of the kayak that you want to turn. That is, on the right side to turn right or vice versa. The bow rudder is often used in place of the telemark turn and is a most effective technique.

Sweep stroke

The sweep stroke is used to turn the kayak round virtually on the spot. Two or three sweeps will usually accomplish this. It can be used as a partial sweep for manoeuvring among obstructions, or for holding a straight course against

Sweep stroke—starting position

Sweep stroke—mid-point

crosswinds. The full sweep is made by placing the paddle blade in the water vertically and directly ahead of the paddler. The paddle is then swept in an arc to directly abeam of the paddler and continued around to directly astern of the paddler.

Reverse sweep
The reverse sweep technique is the opposite to the sweep technique.

In most of the above photographs of paddle strokes, the blades have been deliberately left higher out of the water than in actual practice. This has been done in an attempt to make the stroke clearer to the reader.

Chapter 6 **Canoe Safety**

Too much emphasis cannot be placed on safety, as, like all
outdoor sports, canoeing has some elements of danger. The
greatest danger in canoeing is that of drowning and the largest
contributing factors in the tragic toll of drownings in all
water sports, are panic, exhaustion and ignorance.
Thankfully, fatal accidents in canoeing are very rare, but
nevertheless accidents do happen, and this chapter
outlines the main danger points and how these dangers
can be minimised.

Flooded rivers
The potential danger of a flooded river is beyond estimation.
Unfortunately most of the danger is hidden to the
inexperienced eye, and therefore on no account should
inexperienced paddlers paddle on their own in a flooded river.
The novice should always be in the company of paddlers who
are experienced in this type of water. Be extra careful when
paddling close inshore. Remember that trees growing on the
river bank at normal level are under water when the river
floods. A foot trapped in an underwater tree branch can easily
be fatal, for while you are held securely by the foot, the weight
of water will push your body under.

 If you do capsize in a canoe, keep your body as close to the
surface of the water as possible. Never paddle or attempt to
paddle over a flooded weir. A weir is undoubtedly one of the
most dangerous paddling situations that can confront the
canoeist if not handled properly. When the water drops over a
weir, it creates a turbulence so powerful that if you paddle over
the wall, the water will literally suck you backwards and under
to the bottom of the weir. The correct procedure is to get out
and 'portage' around the weir. Portage is the term used for

70

carrying canoes overland, either between two waterways or around some river hazard.

Eddies

An eddy is a frequent cause of capsize, as it moves in a different direction to the main current in a river. Very often eddies move in a circular motion on the surface of the river and are caused either by a bend in or a narrowing of the river. Paddling into one often leads to your canoe being moved violently sideways. If you are not fast enough in bracing yourself they can throw you off balance and cause you to capsize.

An eddy is always formed on the downstream side of a rock or tree in the river. The water in the eddy is actually moving upstream at this point and therefore can be very useful when paddling up a rapid. Learn to recognise where eddies might be. They can often be identified by the fact that the water in an eddy will be smooth, whereas the rest of the surrounding water will be turbulent.

Vertical eddy

These are much harder to see than a normal eddy and are much more dangerous. They are caused when the current is obstructed by an object, such as a rock, which is either resting on the river bed below the surface, or protruding above the surface. As the name suggests, a vertical eddy moves in a circular or elliptical motion between the river bed and the surface. There are cases on record of canoes being paddled on what appeared to be calm moving water, suddenly being sucked beneath the surface.

Paddler is stationary, facing upstream in an eddy formed by the rock

A kayak under perfect control as it slips downstream in a Grade 2 rapid

Low-level bridges

The biggest danger with a low-level bridge is that the bulk of any floodwater passes under them. This means that, even though there may be 30 to 60 centimetres (1 to 2 feet) of water over them, there is a huge downward motion of water immediately in front of the bridge which can easily pull your canoe beneath the bridge, with disastrous results.

Rapids

A rapid is formed where the river bed slopes downwards, causing the volume of water to run faster than normal. Rapids are graded from 1 to 6 and there are varying interpretations of them. The gradings listed below can be taken as a fair guide:

Grade 1   Slow moving water. Can be handled by any canoe.

Grade 2   Faster moving water. Small open rapids and small drops. Spray cover not essential, although small amounts of water may come inboard. Can be negotiated by any canoe and limited technique.

Grade 3   Rapids may have obstacles, water confused, and
heavier water. A spraysheet is essential. Paddler must be able
to read the water and have a good knowledge of technique.
Canoe must be under control at all times. Water not
dangerous to life.

Grade 4   Heavy, dangerous and confused water. Rapid may
have drops of over a metre. Paddler should be able to Eskimo
roll and have an advanced knowledge of technique.
Experienced paddlers only. Crash hats advised. Water may be
dangerous to life.

Grade 5   Very difficult rapids. Drops of over 1.2 metres
(4 feet). For experts only. Eskimo rolling ability essential.
Very dangerous obstacles. Self-rescue may be possible.
Definitely dangerous to life.

Grade 6   Possible in theory only. Should never be attempted.
Rivers are usually graded by the most difficult rapid, or they
may be split up into sections with a range of gradings. Grade
2-3 would indicate a moderate river, but some rapids would
require reasonable experience and technique. Grade 3-4
would indicate a difficult river suitable for experienced
paddlers only.

Before attempting to shoot any rapid, a careful inspection
should be made. The drop in river height may hide tricky falls
or some other dangerous obstacle that cannot be observed
adequately from a canoe. If you have any doubts about your
ability to shoot a particular rapid safely, do not hesitate to
portage the rapid, or rope your boat down from the river bank.

A change in river height of only a few centimetres can make a
rapid completely different than expected. Make a habit of
checking river heights before setting off on a trip. When
approaching a rapid, look for the smooth vee of water that
indicates the deepest and fastest channel to enter by.

Unless you can Eskimo roll, do not attempt to right your
canoe in a rapid if you capsize. In the event that you do capsize,
slide out of the cockpit, stay with your boat, and float down the
rapid on your back. Always remember to go feet first. Your feet
will absorb an impact with a rock, your head won't.

Avoid overhanging trees—it is very easy to become tangled in
them. Learn to recognise the telltale mound of water that
indicates a submerged obstacle. When following a fellow

73

paddler down a rapid, make sure he is well clear before you go down. Being rammed while side on to a rock or stump is not funny. It is very dangerous and every precaution should be taken to avoid such an incident. Always try and plan your path through a rapid before you actually reach it. Then try to follow this plan when you are in the rapid. If there are very large pressure waves or 'haystacks' which you feel may capsize you, paddle to one side of them rather than down the centre.

The first wave you will encounter on a rapid is called the 'stopper'. This is because it will stop you, or at least slow you down considerably. You must learn to handle your boat in various sizes of stopper wave. A large stopper can be quite dangerous as the bulk of the water is pushing back upstream, while the water below the surface is flowing downstream.

To successfully break through the stopper wave you will need to be travelling quite fast. As you enter it, do not stop paddling unless it is too high to paddle through. Approach it as close to square on as you can. If you capsize in a stopper and find yourself caught in the trough in front of it, dive deep to reach the water travelling downstream.

To do this you may have to remove your buoyancy vest and run the risk of needing it farther along the rapid. If you can, throw your vest over the top of the wave—you may possibly retrieve it farther down the river. Hopefully this course of action may not be necessary; you should make a couple of attempts to dive with your vest on and resort to ditching it only if all else fails. Fortunately, these situations are rare.

Before attempting rapids rated above Grade 2, or before you go canoe surfing, it is very wise to equip your kayak or Canadian with a spraysheet. This can be made either from vinyl coated material or neoprene rubber. The latter is regarded as the best material to use. Spraysheets should be fitted properly. On occasions they may need to be released in a hurry.

Always watch for air bubbles in the water at the bottom of a fall. They indicate that the water has a low specific gravity and will not support a swimmer—another good reason to always stay with a capsized boat.

Your boat should be fitted with 'rescue loops' bow and stern. These should be big enough to get your hand into easily. Fitted to one of them, usually the stern, should be about 6

74

metres (20 feet) of nylon line which can be used to rope your boat down a rapid. This line should be coiled in the boat, away from your feet. It is easier to catch the line in the event of capsize than to try and grab a rescue loop.

A rapid therefore should be the subject of careful assessment. Take the advice of experts and learn from them the art of reading a river. Always participate in club training and instructional days to improve your ability.

While paddling down rapids is great fun, paddling up them will really test your skill and judgment. Always remember not to rush at a rapid. Plan your path before you start, taking note of any obstructions, direction of river flow and the volume of water. The correct technique is to paddle from eddy to eddy. To do this you will have to make great use of ferry gliding, draw strokes and telemark turns and on occasions the slap support. These techniques were explained in earlier chapters.

Rescues

During your canoeing career there will no doubt be many occasions when you will have to 'rescue' a paddler. A rescue race is often a feature of many canoe club carnivals. It is a good idea to practise rescues whenever you get the opportunity, for the time may come when it has to be done in an emergency to save a life. There are many rescue techniques. Here are just a few:

Canadian canoe rescue
It is relatively easy for two persons in a Canadian canoe to quickly and efficiently rescue a third person from the water and right his upturned boat. The person being rescued can be brought over the bow, the stern or the gunwales. If the person is brought over the gunwales, balance is very important, for you can easily find yourself in the water too.

If a person to be rescued is conscious and calm, the easiest method is to paddle up alongside him and let him support himself by hanging on to the gunwale. Keeping your weight slightly on the side opposite the swimmer to counteract the roll of the canoe as his full weight bears down on it, grasp him beneath the armpit with one hand, and with the other hand grasp his shorts and lift him into the canoe. Being conscious he

Classic example of vee approach in rapid. These occur in all rapids to a greater or lesser degree

will be able to assist. If you have a partner, he does the same thing on the other side. As the swimmer comes inboard shift your weight back to the centre of the canoe to prevent it rolling over the opposite side.

If the person is unconscious the same method can be used, but speed is essential. One of you may have to get into the water to assist by grasping the gunwales with one hand while using the other hand to lift the person out of the water. In this case balance is very important, as there is only one person in the canoe to prevent a capsize. Mouth to mouth resuscitation (expired air resuscitation—E.A.R.) should be started immediately, and if necessary external cardiac massage (E.C.M.). See chapter 9 on first aid.

To empty a capsized Canadian canoe in deep water from another canoe, you and your partner should lean over the side and grasp *one* side of the capsized canoe only. Do not attempt to lift the canoe out of the water bodily. Instead, lift one side to break the vacuum, then lift the canoe out of the water and roll it onto an even keel. Another method is to swing the capsized canoe to a position at right angles to your own canoe. It is then possible for one person to empty it, while the other person steadies the canoe. Lift the end of the capsized canoe to break the vacuum, then lay it on the gunwales of your own canoe. Carefully and steadily pull the canoe onto yours until it is free of water. Turn it over and slide it back over the side.

Kayak rescue
To empty a capsized kayak, carefully manoeuvre two kayaks so that they are at right angles to the bow and stern of the capsized kayak. The two paddlers then grasp an end, roll the boat slightly to break the vacuum on the cockpit, then lift slowly, allowing the water to drain out. Restore the boat to the water, so that the empty boat is lying alongside and between the two rescuing kayaks. The paddler can then get back in over the end while his boat is being steadied by his rescuers.

   A kayak can be emptied by one person in another kayak by using the second method described above for Canadians. This method is of course much more difficult and so it is advisable to practise it.

The rescue roll   On many occasions a paddler may capsize and be rescued without getting out of his boat, particularly if he has a spraysheet in place. With practice this method has the advantage that it saves a lot of time and may save a long swim. The paddler after capsizing indicates that this rescue is possible by bringing his hands to the surface and hitting the upturned hull of his kayak with both hands. The nearest paddler to him comes to his assistance by paddling in at right angles to the capsized kayak, placing the bow of his boat as close as possible to the capsized paddler's hand. The paddler under water should be able to see or feel his rescuer's hull and will grasp the bow of his boat and pull himself upright.

Rescue roll—completion stage. Rescuing paddler maintains balance and position by paddling forward and bracing when necessary. Capsized paddler rights himself on the bow of the rescuing kayak

Other safety measures

Never wrap your feet around gear or thwarts in your canoe
when paddling. They could become fouled in the event of a
capsize. Be especially careful with ropes. Always wear a
buoyancy vest when canoeing. The experts wear them, so it is
wise to follow their example. *Never* wear heavy boots or gum
boots in a boat of any kind. Sandshoes or gym boots are best for
boating generally, preferably with holes in the uppers to drain
water.

All canoes should be fitted with adequate fixed buoyancy.
Adequate of course means enough to support both crew and
equipment should the canoe be swamped. Buoyancy can take
many different forms. Sealed empty plastic detergent bottles are
popular, so is polystyrene ('Coolite'). Polyurethane is a two-
part chemical compound which makes excellent buoyancy.
Equal parts of each compound are mixed in a can and
immediately poured into the end of the canoe. It froths up and
solidifies quickly, leaving a block of buoyancy the exact shape
of the bow and stern ends of the canoe. An ordinary car or
motor-cycle tube is also good if you are not carrying too much
gear. It should be pushed in behind the seat and inflated while
inside the canoe.

You can now buy a set of airbags made from heavy duty vinyl
plastic which suit most kayaks. These are pushed into the bow
and stern of the kayak and inflated. They take up most of the
available space, making them ideal for surf canoeing. If gear
has to be carried while using airbags it should be placed on the
bag which can then be inflated around it.

Built-in buoyancy tanks are not a very sound proposition,
although this depends on the individual. In the event of holing
your canoe forward of the buoyancy bulkhead, the
compartment fills up with water and so you lose your
buoyancy. It also compounds the problem of patching as the
patches have to be external.

It is becoming relatively common to see two adults in the
cockpit of a one-man kayak, or an adult and a child. This is an
extremely dangerous practice. In a capsize, two people trying to
struggle out of a small cockpit could easily result in a double
fatality.

The use of a slalom kayak is becoming very popular in

78

the surf, where suitable beaches can be found. Special surf kayaks have been designed and a new sport of kayak surfing is developing. It is great fun, but be very careful and keep away from swimmers and surfers on boards. A wetsuit is an advantage, as a long swim through cold seas can be very exhausting, especially when you are towing a canoe. There is always the danger of hypothermia (exposure), the symptoms of which are almost impossible to detect. It is fatal if not treated immediately.

You may find yourself in the unenviable position of having all your clothing completely soaked on a trip; remember that wet wool is warmer than wet cotton.

Safety in a canoe is basically common sense, and if you adhere to the main safety measures you will have many years of safe, happy canoeing in front of you.

Chapter 7 Eskimo Rolling

In recent years there has been a growing awareness both here and overseas of the value of the Eskimo roll. This chapter covers the basic movements and preliminary technique of the three main rolls — 'put across', 'pawlata' and 'screw'. But first let's look at the reasons for learning the roll.

The first and most obvious reason is to enable the paddler in a capsize to right his boat and continue on his way without having to get out, swim to shore, empty the boat and be on his way again. Also important is the confidence a paddler gets once he has mastered the roll, knowing that he can handle his craft under difficult conditions. Obviously you will not learn to roll merely by reading this book. It requires a great deal of practice, confidence in yourself which can only be gained from constant practice, and a certain amount of tuition from someone who can roll.

While all canoes are not ideal for rolling, it will be found that once the technique has been mastered you will be able to roll in almost any boat. It is quite possible for two men working in close co-ordination to roll a Canadian canoe. However, for the purpose of learning, you should try to use a canoe with a narrow beam. All slalom kayaks and narrow beamed tourers are suitable for learning, provided they are fitted with an adequate spraysheet.

There should also be some means provided of holding yourself in the cockpit when upside down. The average slalom cockpit is small enough to allow you to wedge yourself in by holding your knees and thighs under the cockpit combing. Because a tourer has a larger cockpit, or with a small paddler in a slalom, it may be necessary to find some other method. A piece of 50 x 25-millimetre (2 x 1 inch) timber just long enough to catch under the combing on either side is suitable and

80

will be quite easy to remove if you have to get out in a hurry. It should fit across your lap close to the stomach.

In order to help sort out some of the initial problems, you should use paddles that you are familiar with. I personally prefer flat bladed paddles for learning, as curved blades cause too much confusion to start with. The blades should be feathered at 90 degrees.

In the interests of safety your canoe should have adequate buoyancy. Learning should be done in calm clean water. A swimming pool would be ideal. Although a lot of paddlers learn to roll without the aid of goggles, if you feel they will help you learn, there is no reason why you shouldn't use them. When you have successfully rolled once or twice they should be discarded.

It can be quite discouraging if after many serious attempts to Eskimo roll you are still not successful. If this happens there could be several reasons, the main two being a subconscious fear of being trapped in the boat, and not being sure what you are doing once you are upside down. Both can be overcome with practice.

Although the put across method is generally regarded as the easiest roll to learn, it does not necessarily follow that you will find it the easiest. I first taught myself the pawlata, or something that resembled the pawlata. Before you start to think seriously about Eskimo rolling it is a good idea to overcome thoroughly any anxiety you might have about being trapped in your boat by practising capsizes and then getting out of the boat. First release your spraysheet, then place both hands on the cockpit combing just forward of your hips and push yourself away from the boat. Try this a few times, then gradually increase the time you stay in the boat before getting out. You will find that from a capsized position you can actually swim yourself to the surface and breathe while you are still in the boat. With a little practice you will be able to swim with the boat to shore, dragging it behind you.

The basic theory of how a roll can be done is that the paddle blade is placed flat on the surface of the water and the paddle shaft is used as a bar to pull yourself up on. Also, before you learn to roll, try capsizing your boat in relatively shallow water,

81

then place the paddle vertically on the river bed and climb back up it. Although I normally use this idea for practice and familiarisation, I have had occasion to use it in shallow fast running water with some success.

The put across roll

While sitting in your kayak and before commencing the actual roll, try these practice steps:

1 From the normal paddling position, shift your grip on the paddle so that you have the tip of the left blade in your left hand. The blade should be vertical.

2 Grip the paddle shaft with your right hand and lay the right hand blade *flat* on the surface of the water.

3 Lean yourself and the canoe to the right, and press down sharply with the right hand paddle blade. This action will return you to the normal position.

4 Keep on leaning further and further over to the right and righting yourself by the method described in step 3.

The roll
If you keep practising step 4 above, you will eventually find yourself upside down and returning to the surface. It will be even easier if you lean forward, as this reduces the resistance you present to the water. Now, try letting go of the paddle while upside down, resume your grip, and return to the surface.

When you have mastered this, sit in your kayak in the normal paddling position, turn the left hand blade vertical and capsize to the left. Pause and count three, lean forward, grip your paddle as in steps 1 and 2 above, push the right hand blade to the surface, pull down sharply and complete the roll.

Failure could be caused by one of several factors:

Your paddle is not at right angles to the boat.

You are not leaning forward.

Your right hand paddle blade is not flat when it reaches the water surface, thus causing the blade to slice through the water.

You are not pulling down sharply enough on the right hand paddle blade.

Confusion when capsized. (A face mask or goggles could help you here.)

The pawlata roll

The pawlata roll differs from the put across roll in that where the put across relies on the resistance of the paddle blade to downward pressure, the pawlata works on the action of the blade mounting to the surface.

While sitting in the normal paddling position, take the tip of the left blade in your left hand and hold the paddle shaft in your right hand. The right hand blade should lie flat on the water

84

surface, at right angles to the kayak. Now move the paddle blade forward in an arc towards the bow of the kayak. The leading edge of the blade should be slightly higher than the trailing edge. The blade should move through an arc of approximately 45 degrees. Then move the blade backwards towards the stern through 90 degrees, lifting the leading edge slightly. Notice how the action of lifting the leading edge causes the blade to mount towards the surface.

Pawlata roll—starting position. Note position of right hand

Practise this motion until it can be done quickly and you get used to lifting the leading edge. All this requires is a quick flick of the wrist. (See 'Sculling for support' in chapter 5.) When you can continue this back and forth motion easily and rapidly, lean over to the right and bring yourself back to a vertical position by pressing down with your right hand. The paddle should be in motion all the time.

The roll

Sit in your kayak with your paddle lying along the boat, left hand gripping left hand paddle blade (behind you). It should be vertical. Lean forward and grip the paddle shaft with your right hand. The backs of both hands should face outboard. Capsize and count three, then lean forward. Push the paddle horizontally towards the surface with the outboard edge of the free blade tilted slightly up.

Keep your right arm straight and in one continuous motion sweep your right hand away from the kayak, and push your left hand forward and up towards the surface. When the paddle is at right angles to the kayak you should be nearly upright. Drop both wrists quickly to reverse the tilt of the blade, lean forward hard and push forwards. This should bring you back to the normal vertical position. The pawlata is a roll that requires constant practice as it is easy to slip into the wrong technique. If you fail to roll up, use the put across and try again.

If you fail, check to see if you have incorporated one of the following faults:

Angle of blade wrong. The forward edge *must* tilt up.
Not leaning forward. There is a natural tendency to lean backwards.
Not pushing left hand forward and up.
Movements too slow and unco-ordinated.
Not reversing blade tilt on the return stroke.
Not keeping your right arm straight in the initial sweep.
Trying to roll up before capsize settles. Remember to count three.

The screw roll

Once you have mastered the technique of the pawlata roll, you will probably find the screw roll relatively easy. Its advantage is that your hands don't move very much from your normal

Screw roll—starting position. Note position of paddler's wrists

paddling position. When you become proficient they won't have to be moved at all.

Sit in your kayak with the paddle alongside you and grip the *shaft* with your left hand near the blade and behind you. Lean forward and grip the shaft with your right hand as far forward as you can reach comfortably. The backs of both hands should face outboard. The blade nearest your right hand should be horizontal.

Capsize your canoe or kayak and follow the technique for the pawlata roll. In the event of a sudden capsize, the only movement necessary is to loosen your grip with your left hand and slide it down the shaft until it reaches the top edge of the blade. Because the length of the lever is reduced, it will be necessary to practise this roll to perfection, even more so when you progress to rolling with no variation in the hand position from normal. Failure to complete the roll will be for the same reasons as for failure with the pawlata.

While the three methods described above are considered the most suitable for canoeists who want to learn to roll, you will find that there will be slight variations from different instructors, any of which you may prefer to implement.

Chapter 8   **Canoe Camping and Touring**

Some of the happiest days of my life (and yours too, I hope) have been spent on the banks of a river after a hard or easy day's paddling, far away from the bustle of the city. There is something magnetic about the countryside that draws me. Maybe it's the sound of the river in the stillness of the night, the millions of stars, the companionship of good friends, or the beauty of the wilderness with its scenery and animal life. Whatever it is, it's there for everyone to enjoy, and a canoeist probably has a better chance of seeing it than most people.

Canoe camping is increasing in popularity. Like all active outdoor sports there are pitfalls which an inexperienced canoeist must learn to avoid. Is your canoe in good condition? Are you adequately prepared if your boat is holed? Many a good time has been spoilt because an inexperienced canoeist, and sometimes even an experienced one, has forgotten to take a comprehensive repair kit, or a boat has been lost because it didn't have adequate buoyancy. Remember always, the boat must have enough fixed buoyancy to support its crew and gear.

Rivers are treacherous at the best of times, therefore a

Buoyancy vest supporting unconscious paddler

buoyancy vest is an essential part of a canoeist's equipment. Care must be taken in selecting one to suit the conditions peculiar to canoeing. The first thing to remember is that a buoyancy vest is just what its name implies. It is not a life jacket. Its function is to aid your swimming and prevent tiredness.

A good buoyancy vest should be lightweight. It is usually made of nylon and filled with a series of gas filled plastic packs or closed cell foam. It should not fit tightly under the armpits as this causes chafing, which can make for a very miserable trip. Try to avoid buying the type which is tied on with tape, or the type which bulges under the neck. Both are uncomfortable.

The Canoe Association or a club will advise you on the type of buoyancy most suitable for your purposes.

Many canoeists buy wetsuits for winter paddling, but again care should be taken in choosing the correct type. Ideally they should not have arms in, and long legs are not necessary either. The 'tube' suit that surfers wear is probably the best. I would not even consider ocean or surf paddling, summer or winter, without a wetsuit and buoyancy vest. But it took two bad experiences for me to learn this.

Now let us consider what clothing to take:

Your clothes will vary of course depending on the season and the duration of the trip. It will also be different if you are at a base camp on a river which is accessible by car. In this instance you can take as much clothing as you like.

As I mentioned earlier, woollen clothing is warmer when wet than cotton or synthetic materials, and many paddlers paddle summer and winter in a sleeveless woollen pullover. Even in summer it is advisable to carry at least one woollen pullover. Because of weight, it is important that all clothing should be considered before you go on a trip, as it must serve any eventuality. Summer storms are not uncommon and it can get very cold. While you are paddling, the cold does not seem to affect you very much, but when you stop to make camp your body cools down and you will need warm clothing.

A nylon parka (or anorak) is light and doesn't take up much room. With a pullover underneath such jackets are very warm. They also give protection from heavy or constant rain, or from the spray on rapids and the sea, and there is much to be said for having the matching trousers, particularly in a Canadian canoe.

The summer sun can turn a good time into a nightmare. Remember to take a T-shirt and a hat. A handkerchief tied around the neck minimises the chance of sunstroke.

Summer clothing would consist of shorts, singlets, T-shirts, woollen pullover, woollen socks, underwear, nylon parka (anorak), hat, and old sandshoes, which should be worn on all occasions when canoeing. The amount of clothing taken depends on the length of the trip.

In winter, more clothing or heavier weight clothing should be taken, and two pullovers could be included. Woollen shirts are good, and an old pair of jeans could be an advantage in really cold weather, but they shouldn't be worn while paddling. Winter is wetsuit time so if you have one, take it. You will be glad you did.

Camping equipment

There is no substitute for a good sleeping bag: it is possibly the most important single item you will take with you. So choose your bag carefully. By far the best sleeping bag is one filled with down or 'super down'. Such bags are exceptionally light. They are not rolled like a kapok filled bag but are pushed into the waterproof bag they come in. When they are in their bag they make a bundle considerably smaller than the cheap kapok filled bags.

An important thing to consider is that a sleeping bag does not generate warmth. The warmth is from your body, which the sleeping bag retains. A feather-filled sleeping bag retains this warmth whereas kapok dissipates it. During the night any moisture in the ground soaks into your sleeping bag, and this is also where the cold comes from. For this reason a waterproof groundsheet should always be used. Kapok takes considerably longer to dry out if you get it wet. Buy yourself a closed cell foam mat. It will serve a dual purpose by giving you something comfortable to sit on while canoeing, and will provide excellent insulation if you sleep on it at night. It has the added advantage of not soaking up water.

Your tent is the next most important item. Even during summer months we get dew, as well as an occasional storm.

You might prefer to sleep under the stars, but it's good to have a tent erected, just in case. There are many excellent tents on the market including a range of good European brands. Up until recently most lightweight tents were made from japara. Now many are nylon, which is lighter still than japara and has a greater water resistance. The tent design for you will be a matter of personal choice.

Some people favour the A tent because it is easy to erect. Many people favour a walled tent because it gives greater head room, although it takes a little longer to put up. A tent with a sewn-in floor has the advantage of being relatively waterproof, but it is a little heavier because of the extra material in it. A tent with a bell end gives you extra space for storing gear, and a tent supplied with its own aluminium poles saves you the trouble of looking for timber before erecting your tent. Whichever type of tent you decide on, it will only give you good service if it is looked after properly.

A tent properly erected should have no creases in the walls or roof, and it should not 'belly' or sag. You should erect it with the flaps closed so that you will not have any trouble closing them properly in the event of a sudden shower. Although many tents are rot resistant, they should not be rolled and stored while damp, but hung up to dry and air first. They should be stored in a cool, well ventilated area, off the floor.

Never put a tent on the ground to sleep on, particularly on sand, as the sand will get into the material fibres and wear them out. Eventually the tent will leak. Always make sure the guy ropes are in good condition and that you have enough tent pegs to put the tent up with. There is nothing quite as frustrating and annoying as to find yourself fishing around for bits of string for guys and using rocks and logs for pegs, especially if you are in a hurry—in the middle of a thunderstorm, for example. Remember that your tent is your home in camp. Treat it with respect, and it will give you many years of service.

How to pick a campsite
Picking a good campsite is not always as easy as it sounds. First, it has to be reasonably accessible to water, but high enough to escape the effects of a flash flood. Try to avoid camping on a riverbank where the valley walls rise steeply close to the river. It

92

is not uncommon for rivers to rise considerably overnight. A depression or gully on otherwise flat ground may be a snug campsite in a high wind, but could form a small lake or creek in heavy rain.

Don't camp on sloping ground if you can help it. Water running down a hillside can make an unpleasant night. Try to find a spot sheltered by trees, but keep away from trees with dead limbs. A small rise is a good spot, although it will be exposed to wind. Water will run off all the way round. If you camp on level ground and there is a chance of rain, dig a drain round your tent before it starts. Always remember to fill these drains in before leaving camp.

It is a good idea to use three pegs on each of your main guys, skewered in at different angles, particularly if your tent is pitched on soft ground. Always try to avoid sand.

Food
There is not a lot of point carrying lightweight gear if you are going to take along huge amounts of canned and fresh foods. A few years ago dehydrated foods were known only to the bushwalking enthusiast travelling light. Now of course they are very popular. These foods prepared properly are very wholesome, filling and contain most of the vitamins, protein and other essential elements that fresh foods have.

A balanced diet is essential no matter what you do in life, but if you are very active it is even more important. Your body needs a certain amount of every vitamin daily. If you are not getting what your body needs you are harming yourself. So plan carefully the food you take. If you feel you are not getting the correct daily allowance of vitamins, there are a number of multivitamin capsules available, which contain the required amount of each vitamin. These are in no way harmful and any excess in vitamins is excreted normally.

Let's have a look at the range of foods available in dehydrated form. First of course there is milk, probably the most common dried food. There are many different brands of dried potatoes, peas, beans, carrots, and onions, as well as packs containing a mixture of two or more vegetables. Dried egg and dried meat are not so common but they are available through stores that supply lightweight camping equipment. Specialist outdoor shops in particular usually stock a very good range of dehydrated foods.

There are many packaged meals which feature rice as the main bulk of the meal, with some form of dehydrated exotic topping that comes along in separate little packets. Packet soups form a nourishing meal or first course, and there is an endless variety of flavours. Rice, though heavier than most dried foods, is a grain that can be used in endless combinations. A small amount can make a big meal. Always carry some as emergency rations.

Porridge has always been my favourite winter breakfast. It is a good warm start to a cold winter day. If you like it can also be served straight from the packet with cold milk and sugar. You can now buy from local stores 'instant' porridge which requires only mixing with hot water. There is certainly no need to eat the same thing over and over again. With a little imagination you can eat as well in camp as at home.

On most canoeing trips, lunch is only a brief stop, or it may even be eaten on the move. For this reason it should be quick and simple. Crispbread in one of its many forms is a good substitute for bread, which is too bulky to carry and goes stale quickly. Cheese, yeast extract, honey, peanut butter and dried fruits all make quick, simple and pleasant lunches. Health food stores carry a range of such things as sunflower seed bars and sesame seed bars which are energy giving foods full of nourishment. Chocolate makes a pleasant finish to a meal and is good for you. Don't forget dried fruits such as apples, pears, apricots and peaches. Stew them for tea, and any left over can be kept to be eaten with your breakfast.

Cooking and cooking equipment

Cooking a good meal in the camp is an art in itself. You will be surprised at what can be accomplished over an open fire with only a little practice.

Often the best results will be obtained from cooking one large appetising hot-pot, putting everything into the saucepan.

There is no real secret to cooking in the open. All it needs is practice. Food should be cooked slowly on a fire comprised mainly of red coals. A large flaming fire is great for a quick cup of tea or to warm yourself by, but it will invariably burn your food. Most dried vegetables need only be brought to the boil and simmered for two or three minutes. Potato needs only the addition of boiling water. Fruit needs to be cooked for a while so that it can absorb water. Rice needs approximately eight cups of water to each cup of rice. Soups should be simmered slowly. Don't forget to add salt to your vegetables as they cook.

When cooking a meal with two or more courses, try to cook so that there is no waiting between courses. It is often better to cook in groups of three or four and combine your food as well as equipment.

Cooking utensils should be light and rustproof, so aluminium is ideal. Buy a saucepan and a frying pan, which can double as a saucepan lid. Teapots, kettles etc. are not necessary. An unbreakable plastic mug, a deep enamelled plate and a set of ordinary stainless steel cutlery is all you will need for eating. Remember to take a sharp knife for cutting bread and a tin opener.

No matter how marvellous it is to have an open fire, there will be times when you want to produce a meal quickly and will need to use a stove. Butane and propane gas stoves are available in camping stores and are fine as long as you are in an area where it is easy to buy refills. However, the paraffin pressure stove is possibly the most convenient and popular with canoeists.

For short expeditions or where fires are not permitted, canoe campers usually take pre-cooked meat on their trips. Substantial meals may be made from cold meat and salad vegetables.

Fires

Even when there are no restrictions on the use of fires, there are certain precautions that must be taken.

Never build a fire where there is dry grass or in close proximity to overhanging tree branches. Clear the area around your fire site for a radius of at least three metres. Surround your fireplace with rocks and keep it out of the wind. Don't build a fire at the base of a tree. A good place is at the foot of a sandy bank, provided there is no grass hanging down over the bank. Don't build a fire any bigger than you need. If there is a possibility of rain overnight, collect some dry firewood before it rains and store it in a tent. The next morning you will have no trouble starting a fire.

Always douse your fire with water before leaving it, and cover it with rocks or sand. Remember fires are dangerous. Treat them with the respect that they deserve.

Hygiene

One of the most important aspects of camping is hygiene, both personal and with cooking and sanitation. There is no excuse for lack of personal hygiene in camp, even if your daily bath consists of nothing more than a brisk rub down with a damp coarse towel. But wherever possible you should bathe daily. There is nothing so refreshing or exhilarating as a bath in a river in the middle of winter. But don't stay in too long.

Take care when cooking and preparing food, especially in summer. Flies are a menace around food. Try to keep all your food covered. All saucepans, plates, etc. should be scrupulously cleaned after each meal, at least on the inside. Bury or burn all your rubbish after each meal. Food cans should be burnt, beaten flat and brought back with you. Remember to leave your campsite as clean or cleaner than you found it.

When getting water for drinking, always take it from a point upstream of your campsite. Unfortunately many of our waterways are polluted, so it is a good idea to use purifying tablets if there is the slightest doubt about the water's freshness. Alternatively, boil the water first, but remember it should boil for a minimum of twelve minutes to be certain of destroying any harmful bacteria.

When travelling through inhabited country it is simpler and safer to collect water from a domestic supply and carry a plastic bottle of it in the canoe.

Keep camp latrines a good safe distance from the river bank. Cover all excreted matter with sand each time you visit the latrine. This will help discourage flies. If you are in a permanent camp, have a good supply of a strong disinfectant in the latrine. These measures are all part of simple basic hygiene but they will help to make your camp both happier and healthier.

Waterproofing your equipment

One of the quickest ways of upsetting your trip is to accidentally capsize, and then find out that your gear was not sufficiently waterproofed. Waterproofing isn't a haphazard business. A little care taken when packing will pay dividends in a capsize.

Waterproofing gear for a Canadian canoe is a lot easier than for a kayak. Canadian paddlers often pack their gear in drums. These are plastic and have a large opening in the top. The top screws on and is usually fitted with a waterproof gasket. There are a number of different sizes of these drums and they are relatively inexpensive. One of the most popular is sold for the making of home-brewed beer.

The equipment shown packed in the canoe was sufficient for two on a seven-day trip. Note baling bucket, camera in plastic container, spare paddle tied in near gunwale, spraysheet alongside canoe

Packing for a kayak should be done carefully. As the storage space in a kayak is usually reached through an opening in the seat, your gear has to be packed in bundles small enough to go through this hole easily. Your gear will probably be in three or four bundles and I have found it is a good idea to tie these together with light line and about 60 centimetres (2 feet) apart. This line can then be tied to the seat.

Since the advent of the 'garbage bag', packing has become somewhat easier. Such bags, together with the heavy gauge plastic rucksack liners which are on sale at most camping equipment stores, will be all the waterproofing you need for normal equipment. First pack your gear in a garbage bag. It's a good idea to carry several as spares. Then tie the open end. Put this inside your rucksack liner and tie the top of it. Then place this inside a bag made from canvas or calico with a draw string in the top. The calico bag will protect your plastic bags from getting torn on any projections you might have inside your boat.

When packing your kayak, you might find you can stow some gear up in the bow, but don't put too much up there and make the bow too heavy or it will tend to nose dive your kayak. It makes paddling pretty hard. Your boat should ride level with you in it, or a little down on the stern. For the sake of manoeuvrability, don't have any heavy gear slopping around in your boat; make sure it is held firmly in place.

Photography

Whether or not you are on a standing camp or touring, photography is an important part of canoeing. The first thing to think of is waterproofing your camera. You can buy underwater cases for most popular brands of camera, but if you don't want to go to this expense, use a plastic bag. Pull the bag tightly across the lens making sure there are no wrinkles and secure it with an elastic band. Press some air out of the bag, fold the end and secure this with an elastic band. You can wind on, press plungers and twiddle knobs quite successfully through the bag. To carry your camera in your boat, use one of the many plastic containers which are now on the market.

One of the main troubles with photographs or slides is that the subject is often posing, and looks as if he is. Try to get unposed shots to catch people being themselves. If you are taking photographs from the bank include part of the bank or tent, or frame the shot with trees. Get people in the foreground to give the photograph character. Use colours to help depth. Reds and orange accede in photographs while blues and greens tend to recede. To get shots underwater make a tube approximately 30 centimetres (1 foot) square with a glass bottom, or use the plastic bag. Add drama to your photography by taking shots from low down in the water or half in and half out of the water.

You have probably experienced the problem of trying to get a photograph with good clarity, where you have a paddler in water on a sunny day. You get so much reflection that it is very difficult to get a light meter reading on the canoeist's skin tone. You usually get a well exposed shot of white water and sky, while the paddler is black, especially if he was in back light. Solve this problem by taking a light reading on your own skin, set your camera on this setting and take your photograph.

If you are taking a photograph from your canoe include the bow of your canoe in it. Carry your camera wherever you go and be ready to get interesting, once in a lifetime shots.

Chapter 9 **First Aid**

On all trips you should carry a first aid kit, and know some elementary first aid. You never know what will crop up and you usually can't ring for a doctor. I am not going to go into great detail with first aid, as there are many excellent aid books available. You should, however, be familiar with the following:

The control of bleeding

Artificial resuscitation, including mouth to mouth resuscitation

How to treat shock

How to render a limb immobile

How to treat exposure (hypothermia)

Snake and spider bite, where these are a danger

External cardiac massage

How to treat burns and scalds, and how to minimise and prevent infection

The most important thing to remember is that in any accident there will be some degree of shock and this will vary with the individual.

Bleeding

No matter what other injuries are present, first stop bleeding. Venous bleeding, indicated by the darkness of the blood and steady flow, is stopped by direct pressure on the wound. Arterial bleeding, when blood spurts from the wound with each heartbeat and is bright red, should be stopped with direct pressure if possible. If this is not possible, stop the flow of blood at the nearest pressure point and apply a constrictive bandage. However, try to avoid the use of a constrictive bandage, which should be a last resort. A tourniquet is the most dangerous method of stopping bleeding and is not recommended, unless in an emergency. In all cases of bleeding, keep the patient quiet

100

and lay him down if possible. If the bleeding is from a limb, elevate it if there is no suspicion of a fracture.

Shock
Learn to recognise the symptoms of shock and the treatment.
Symptoms   Pulse at first slow, then becomes rapid. Dizziness, fainting, the patient may become unconscious. Pupils of the eyes are larger. Skin is pale and cold; sweating and clamminess. Nausea, vomiting and retching.
Treatment   Immediate first aid. Loosen clothing, particularly round the neck. Stop bleeding. Keep the patient warm.
Keep his head level with his heart.
If he is conscious, give him a warm sweet drink, but definitely not alcohol.
Look confident even if you are not and reassure him.

Artificial resuscitation
Mouth to mouth resuscitation is by far the best method of resuscitation and it should be known thoroughly.
1 Lay the patient on his back.
2 Clear his airways; empty his mouth with your finger. The patient's head may be turned on its side to accomplish this.
3 Pull the head back by placing your left hand on his forehead and pressing down while lifting under his neck with your right hand. His head can be left in this position by leaving your left hand in place, and putting a bundle of clothing under his neck. With his neck extended this way his airway will be open.
4 Pinch the nostrils. In the case of a small child, the child's mouth and nose should be covered by your mouth.
5 Blow down the mouth until the chest rises. If it doesn't respond immediately, tilt the head further back. In the case of a small child or baby, the blow down the mouth will be only a small puff.
6 Remove your mouth and watch the chest fall.
7 Continue to breathe for the patient until he can breathe himself or until he is pronounced dead.

External cardiac massage
In order to determine whether the patient's heart is beating,

101

place the pads of the right hand fingers in the groove between the voicebox and the neck muscles, level with the Adam's apple. Press back to feel the carotid artery. If a pulse can be felt, the heart is beating; if it cannot, lift the upper eyelid of the patient's left eye. If the pupil is large and not reacting to light, and a pulse cannot be felt on a second attempt, the heart has stopped beating and external heart massage must be started at once.

The heart is in the centre of the chest behind the breast bone (sternum). If pressure is applied to the lower half of the breast bone, the heart is compressed and blood is pushed into the arteries. When pressure is released the breast bone springs forward. Compression stops and blood flows into the heart from the veins. Rhythmical pressure produces an artificial heartbeat and circulates blood through the body.

Technique

1 The patient is placed on a solid support, not a springy bed.
2 Locate the breast bone.
3 The lower half of the breast bone of an infant is depressed about 12 millimetres ($\frac{1}{2}$ inch) using two or three fingers. The lower half of the breast bone of a child is depressed about 25 millimetres (1 inch) with the heel of one hand.
   The lower half of the breast bone of an adult is depressed 50 millimetres (2 inches) with the heels of two hands, one on top of the other. With an adult it will be necessary to lean directly on the chest, holding the arms straight. Infants and children need very little pressure.
4 Pressure should be applied sixty times per minute.
5 If breathing has stopped as well as the heartbeat, and you are on your own, give fifteen rapid compressions of the chest, and then two breaths of air. This sequence should be repeated three or four times per minute.
6 If there are two of you, one should give mouth to mouth resuscitation, while the other gives external heart massage. Each lung inflation should be followed by five chest compressions. Chest compressions should not be done while lungs are being inflated. This sequence should be repeated twelve times per minute.

Bone fractures

If a broken bone is suspected, splints or bandages will be required. Do not move the patient unless he is in danger from another source. If you are not sure the bone is broken, treat as a break. If you have no equipment, splints or bandages, make sure the limb does not move by placing small heavy articles alongside it. If you do not know how to splint a fracture, send for help and protect your patient. If a broken bone is protruding through the skin, cover it with a clean dressing.

How to recognise a break
Immediate area will be tender and painful.
The patient may lose some degree of use, but don't rely on this.
Some swelling may occur but not necessarily immediately.
Treat for shock.
The limb may be twisted or deformed.
A light touch with the fingers may detect the break or uneven bone.

Immediate treatment
Improvise splints. They must be long enough to stop all movement of the limb.
The injured part may be bandaged to an uninjured part of the body.
Bandaging must be done carefully to avoid moving the injured part.
Do not overtighten bandages.
If you have not learnt the correct treatment, send for help.
Fractures of the neck or back require special training.
Avoid moving the patient and send for skilled help.

Exposure

Exposure is usually brought on by rain, cold, lack of food and weariness. It occurs when the body temperature drops below normal. This is often caused by wearing inadequate clothing. Exposure is not easy to recognise and the sufferer will not recognise it coming on. He will be exhausted, lag behind, be reluctant to carry on, not 'with it' mentally and difficult to reason with. He must be sheltered from the weather. It is necessary for him to put on extra clothing and be given food and drink.

Recovery can be swift, but if it has not occurred within fifteen minutes, or if he has collapsed, he will be past warming himself and will need immediate assistance. He *must* be treated on the spot or he may collapse (if he hasn't already) and die. If possible, change him into dry clothing, put him in a sleeping bag and have a strong member of the party get in with him, or have two fit people both in sleeping bags lie close alongside him. *This is the only safe method. Excessive external heat can kill him.* Do not attempt to rub the patient's skin to warm him; this will only serve to draw warm blood from his vital organs. For a small outlay you can buy a large polyethylene bag or a 'heat sheet' which will completely cover a person suffering from hypothermia. They are extremely effective even if his clothing is wet. At least one member of your party should carry one of these survival aids. Alcohol must not be given. He must not be moved until fully recovered. Make camp immediately and keep an eye on the rest of the party for any similar cases which may occur.

Snakebite

This treatment is advised by the Royal Society of Tropical Medicine and Hygiene.

1 Kill the snake.

2 The commonest symptoms are shock and fear of death. Convincing reassurance is vital at all stages. Death from snakebite is rare.

3 Keep the patient at rest.

4 Apply a lightly constricting ligature. Use a handkerchief or piece of cloth to occlude veins and lymphatics draining the bitten area (but not the arteries). This must be released for one minute in every thirty.
Soft rubber tubing applied over clothing to minimise bruising makes an excellent ligature. Release for one minute in every thirty as above.

5 Wash the bitten surface with clean water without rubbing.

6 Immobilise the bitten part as for a fracture and if possible keep it in a dependent position (i.e. hanging down).

7 Administer analgesics (e.g. aspirin) but not morphia.

8 Call a doctor or transfer to hospital (with the dead snake, if available).

Spider bite
Deal with as for snakebite.

Burns
Immediately soak in cold water or apply ice packs if available. If small the burns should be covered with a sterile cloth and loosely bandaged. Do not apply any ointment or lotions and take every precaution not to break any blisters that may have formed. If the burns are large, and there is burnt clothing adhering to them, leave clothing alone. Cover loosely and seek medical aid. Treat for shock and keep the patient warm and rested.

Infection
This should be guarded against at all costs. Wash hands before treating any wound. Clean any foreign material from the wound with clean, boiled water if no antiseptic is available. Do not apply antiseptic without first reading the directions printed on the bottle. Always dilute with water before use. Keep wounds covered.

No matter what your vocation, a good sound knowledge of first aid could save a life. It may even be your own. The following books are recommended as additional reading to increase your knowledge:

First Aid, the authorised manual of the St John Ambulance Association or of the Red Cross

It is recommended that a first aid book and a well equipped first aid kit be carried on all trips.

Appendix

Further reading
XXX   *Better Canoeing* by Alan Harber. Kaye and Ward, London.
XX   *Living Canoeing* by Alan Byde. A. & C. Black, London.
XX   *Canoe Building* by Alan Byde. A. & C. Black, London.
XXX   *Canoeing Complete* by Brian Skilling. Kaye and Ward, London.
XX   *Canoe Cruising Manual* by Noel McNaught. Kaye and Ward, London.
X   *Canoeing Waters* by P. W. Blandford. Lutterworth Press, Guilford, Surrey.
XX   *Sea Canoeing* by Derek Hutchinson. Ocean Publications, London.
XX   *Guide to the Waterways of the British Isles* by British Canoe Union. 70 Brompton Road, London, SW3 1DT.
XXX   *Kayaking* by Jay Evans and Robert Anderson. Stephen Greene Press, Vermont.
XX   *Whitewater Sport* by P. Dwight Whitney. Ronald Press, New York.
XX   *Canoeing* by American National Red Cross. Washington.

Special merit   XXX
Very sound   XX
Useful   X

National Associations in Britain and America
British Canoe Union:
  70 Brompton Road,
  London, SW3 1DT
  (has Divisions in Scotland, Wales and Northern
  Ireland)

Irish Canoe Union:
  c/o Venture Sports,
  Rockhill, Black Rock,
  Co. Dublin

Canadian Canoe Association:
  333 River Road,
  Vanier Place,
  Vanier City,
  Ontario K1L 8B9

American Canoe Association:
  189 Prairie Street,
  Concord Mass. 01742

Federation Mexicana de Canotaje:
  Sanchez Ascona 1348
  Mexico 12, D.F.

International Canoe Federation (ICF):
  G. Massaia 59,
  50129 Florence, Italy.

British Canoe Union Coaching Scheme
The Coaching Scheme is administered by the National
Coaching Committee and the country has been divided
into areas with a coaching panel in each area, managed
by Area Coaching Organisers assisted by the coaches and
instructors in the area. They will control the coaching
activities, offering a valuable service to anyone who
desires advice, instruction or testing in canoeing skills and
taking responsibility for organising courses and
examinations for potential coaches and instructors.

The British Canoe Union has devised tests of proficiency in the correct handling of canoes and kayaks. There are three standards:
1 The Elementary Canoeist Test (Canadian or Kayak)
2 Inland Proficiency Test (Canadian or kayak)
3 Sea and Open Water Proficiency Test (Kayak)
4 Inland Advanced Test (Canadian and Kayak)
5 Advanced Sea Test (Kayak)

There are also B.C.U. Coaching Awards:
1 Senior Instructor Award (Inland, Sea, Canadian)
2 Coach Award
3 Senior Coach Award
4 Specialist Coach Award (Racing, Slalom, Sailing, etc.)

The British Canoe Union Corps of Canoe Lifeguards
The purpose behind this organisation is to provide competent canoeists with opportunities to apply their skills in service to the community. Amongst the aims are:
1 To set a high standard of canoemanship in canoe skills, approach to water safety and boat maintenance.
2 To be available to assist Local Authorities or Police in times of flood; provide safety patrols at regattas; patrol beaches during the summer months.
3 To offer demonstrations of canoeing techniques, and to act as qualified instructors to groups of canoeists, especially in schools and youth clubs.
4 To lead or accompany canoe expeditions made by schools or youth clubs, both at home and abroad.
Membership of a Canoe Lifeguard Unit is accepted as a qualification for the Public Service Section of the Duke of Edinburgh's Award Scheme.

Individual canoeists can become Full Members of the BCU and canoeing clubs can affiliate to it.

All enquiries about membership or services should be addressed to the Administrator at the Headquarters in Brompton Road, London.

Glossary of Canoeing Terms

abeam (of paddler)   A point at 90 degrees to the length of a canoe or kayak, and in line with the paddler

astern   Towards the stern

beam   Distance across the gunwale in a Canadian canoe at its widest point. Distance across the widest point of a kayak

bow   Front end of a boat or ship

buoyancy   Flotation material to prevent sinking

C.1   Canadian canoe: one man

C.2   Canadian canoe: two men

combing or cockpit   Raised edge around a kayak cockpit

crash hat   Safety headgear used by paddlers in rapid or white water

feather   Refers to feathered paddle blades. Paddle blades (kayak) with different planes, usually at between 75 and 90 degrees

forward   Towards the bow

gunwale   Top edge of a Canadian canoe

hull   The shell of the boat excluding any deck

K.1   Kayak: one man

K.2   Kayak: two men

K.4   Kayak: four men

painter   Length of light rope attached to the bow or stern (or both) of a canoe

portage   To carry a canoe and equipment around an obstacle, e.g. rapid, tree blockup, etc

race   Shallow fast moving water over gravel or river stone, or slope in river bed

rescue loop   Handhold on bow and stern of canoe

rubbing strips   Timber strips usually fitted to the hull of a canvas canoe to prevent wear

rudder   Steering equipment used mainly on racing kayaks

spraysheet or spraydeck   Removable fabric or rubberised waterproof sheet, fitted around a paddler's waist and around the cockpit of a kayak. In Canadian canoes spraysheets are usually secured with press studs around the gunwales

stern   Back end of a boat or ship

thwart   Cross-member between gunwales in Canadian canoe, usually constructed of timber

weir   Retaining wall across a river, used to control river height and flow

DATE DUE			
NOV 6 '78			
MAY 14 '79			
DEC 19 '80			
APR 24 '89			
OCT 16 '89			

30 505 JOSTEN'S